David Henderson's Dog Stories
A Collection

Foreword by
Joel Vance

Illustrations by
Shep Foley

Winchester Press
An imprint of New Win Publishing, Inc.

Credits

The author is indebted to the editors and the publishers of the magazine and the publications where some of these stories previously appeared. Among such works are *Gun Dog Magazine, Retriever Journal, Pointing Dog Journal, Wing and Shot, Wildlife in North Carolina, Lyons Publishing* and *New Win Publishing*. While initial publication was "first rights" only, in each instance I have currently received encouragement and good wishes for this little book.

I am also indebted to daughters Shep Foley for painstaking illustrations and jacket, and Anne Henderson for graphic aid. (And to both for help and comfort on family health problems.)

Copyright © 1998 by David H. Henderson
and Shepard H. Foley

Printing Code 11

Library of Congress Cataloging-in-Publication Data

Henderson, David H.
   David Henderson's dog stories : a collection / [David Henderson] ;
foreword by Joel Vance ; illustrations by Shep Foley.
    p. cm.
  ISBN 0-8329-0516-X
  1. Dogs--Fiction. I. Title.
PS3558.E4828D38 1998
813'.54--dc21   98-39315
                                      CIP

Printed in the United States of America

Contents

This book is dedicated to the dogs, all sorts of dogs, and those who love them and love to read about them.

The illustrations by Shep Foley have captured the essence of the special rapport between us and our dogs and we wish to give her our thanks for her dedication to this effort.

The Publisher

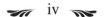

Foreword

 s I write, nine French Brittany puppies are trying
to get their legs under them in the next room, their
just-opening eyes glimmering at the new world
they've moved to.

I'm a sucker for dogs. When I was a kid, the collies of
Albert Payson Terhune were more real than most of the
people I knew and I lived with Jack London's fabled dogs
in the frozen North.

Now, as an adult, David Henderson's dogs similarly
capture my imagination and set fire to my emotions.

I have bird dogs, primarily for bobwhite quail, though
they've performed admirably on just about all the North
American game birds.

But dogs are dogs, regardless of specialty, each with
personality and each with something to offer us. They are
not people, but we share many common traits with them.

My dogs live to hunt, eat and make love. Who has the audacity to call them inferior creatures.

Do dogs have memory and do they think? Of course they do. A dog can remember the location of something awful it rolled in for years. And if it "thinks" you would disapprove, it will concoct elaborate schemes to divert your attention while it rolls in the awful substance again.

There's an apocryphal story about a man checking into a motel with a dog. "I can vouch for my dog," says the fellow, "if you'll let him stay with me in the room."

"Mister," says the motel owner, "I've never had a dog steal towels, bedclothes, silverware or pictures off the wall. I've never had to evict a dog for being drunk and I've never had a dog run out on the bill.

"Yes, your dog is welcome and if your dog will vouch for you, you're welcome too."

I'll vouch for Dave Henderson and his dogs, so, come along and meet unforgettable dogs and the people they own.

Joel Vance
August 1998

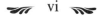

Prologue and Soliloquy

hese tales are simply stories about dogs—all kinds of dogs. Definitely not hunting stories, but because I know best those breeds, the bird dogs like fine cream, come to the top as protagonists. Many of the stories actually were dreamed up, i.e., the plots come in the night with just enough left over for me to set down some sort of clues on paper before the dream faded. I think of this collection as a celebration of almost seventy years of Dave and dog.

Like William Faulkner on receiving the Nobel for literature, I wrote them "not for glory and least of all for profit, but to create out of the materials of the human spirit something which did not exist before." If this sounds unctuous or presumptuous, it's because I have set a very high regard for the subject, born of long association with dogs of every strain. There is some humor here, but also, I hope, some insight into the mystery of man's love affair with his dog which has gone on for a long, long time.

Almost as long, man has written about the creature. One of the early quotes comes from Socrates, "The more I see some men, the more I like my dog," or words to that effect. Herodotus acknowledged that "in whatever house a cat has died by a natural death, all those who live in the house shave their eyebrows only; but those in whose house a dog has died shave their whole bodies." Some honor, huh? Hereafter, I have accumulated hundreds of words of eulogies from which I'll retrieve that which I think may interest you, but shall pass on in no chronological order.

Judges seem to have a particularly intense desire to recognize the rare traits of canine/human relationship.

Perhaps they only want to show off in written opinions that will permanently honor, not only the subject, but the author. I shall take advantage of such judicial scholarship (and the fact that these writings are in the public domain) to draw heavily on at least two such collections. Without specifically crediting each quotation, I should mention two sources: the first is the opinion of Justice Sterling Price Gilbert in the case of <u>Montgomery vs. Maryland Casualty</u>, on appeal from 39 Ga. App 210, 1930. (I do not have the Sup. Ct. citation, but the case involved an employee's unsuccessful attempts to get workman's compensation for trying to save a "fellow worker," the night watchman's dog, which had fallen overboard and was drowning.) After going back to the "dawn of primal history," his honor said, "We find in astrology the dog star that is the brightest star in the Heavens: the Alpha of the constellation Canis Major, and in Greek mythology Cerberus is the watch dog at the entrance to the infernal regional." He goes on to describe the welcome afforded Ulysses by his dog Argos, full of fleas who 'wagged this tail and dropped his ears,' but could not closer reach his master and died the black death. The English painter Landseer brought Argos immortality on canvas.

From the Bible, "a living dog is better then a dead lion" Ecclesiastes IX:4. Many French writers take credit for "who loves me, loves my dog." One of my favorites is from the English Lord Byron, who wrote of 'Boatswain:'

> But the poor dog, in life the firmest friend,
> The first to welcome, foremost to defend,
> Whose honest heart is still his master's own,
> Who labors, fights, lives, breathes for him alone.

Boatswain, wrote Byron, "possessed beauty without vanity, strength without insolence, courage without ferocity and all the virtues of man without his vices."

For years people have denigrated cross-bred dogs by referring to them as "curs." It would interest you to know that there is now a National Cur and Feist Breeders' Association that extols the virtues of "Mountain Curs," "Black Mouth Curs" and "Stephen's Stock." Mountain curs are frequently born with an extra dew claw on each hind foot...which often form additional functional toes. (See what you'll learn if you read.)

The second judicial source of maybe more than you want to know about dogs was written by my good friend, Judge

Harry C. Martin, Jr. of the North Carolina Court of Appeals in State of North Carolina vs. James E. Wallace, N.C. App. 271 S. E. and 760 back in 1980. The state had foolishly continued a charge against Wallace for running deer with a dog—charges stupidly brought under a motor-vehicle statute. But Harry took offense and put Judge Gilbert in no better than second place, both in length and depth of juridical recognition of dogs' place in men's life.

He cites the huntress Diana with the dogs given by Pan and continues to track Gilbert. But than, on his own, he tells of the spaniel that saved William of Orange from the Spaniards, the gallant deeds of the St. Bernards in the Alps, and squeezed a tear at the picture of a boy without a dog. He digs out old cases that created "one free bite" for dogs, including one that says you can't shoot a neighbor's dog, simply because it looks hungrily at your chickens safe behind your fence.

Judge Martin is not content with local deification. He quotes from a Kentucky court, "History may have searched in vain to find a living creature exhibiting so much fidelity and affection as does the dog for his master. Neither cold, heat, danger nor starvation deters him (sic) manifesting those most excellent qualities for his master." He (Martin) found a New York case where a butcher, paying off a drover with a bank note, had the note fall into a gravy dish. The drover's dog ate the note. The demand that the dog be dissected was refused. Now the comedy: the butcher claimed that the dog had collected his master's account, while the drover insisted that the dog was not acting within the scope of his duties and authorities and sued the butcher.

Then Judge Martin picks up the most quoted eulogy on dogs of all time—the comments of Senator Vest in the Missouri case of Burden vs. Hornsby. It is an essay in itself, too long for here. Go to the library and read it. "When all other friends desert, he remains. When riches take wings and reputation falls to pieces, he is as constant in his love as the sun on its journey through the heavens."

This is the dog. This is our friend and companion who inspires great literature, great art, and even short stories that pop into this writer's head in the dead of night.

I hope you'll like therm.

X

Red Dog Retriever

have always taken pride in being known as a sto-
ryteller. Here at 80, and in an era of cyberspace,
whatever that is, I may be one of the last to pass on
verbally the tales told to me by my father, and his before
him. But before time calls the coda on this life, I need to
record the story of the great red dog. And what she did to
deserve it.

Actually, it was told to me many times by my dad, her
heroics having occurred shortly before I was born. But if you
keep reading, you'll see why I have cause for gratitude.

"Once upon a time," he'd say, "there was a boy who lived
by the sea." And, of course, I'd know that boy was my dad.
Then he'd tell how he grew up in the village of Chester on
the North Carolina coast. Actually, it faced on Core Sound,
named for the Core Indian tribe found there by the first
English colonists. Every Chesterman was a waterman, making a living fishing or guiding for ducks and geese in season.
And many a time, out of season as well, back in the day of
market hunters.

But also, every man at one time or another in his life, served in the U.S. Life Saving Service, (later the U.S. Coast Guards). For just south lay the famous Cape Lookout, and the Core Banks and Lookout shoals that were almost as deadly to shipping as the "graveyard of the Atlantic" further north at Cape Hatteras. And a surfman received $65 a month, cash, for the ten danger months, although he had to pay for his uniform and keep. Still, this was far better than most residents of Carteret County earned at the turn of the century. And my Dad, about twenty in the early 1900's, was a surfman in District 6.

This, though, is the story of a dog, and how she came to be a part of the crew.

Dad said that he had lived for two winters up near the Virginia line, guiding for rich Northerners who had built hunting lodges at Knott's Island, Corolla, and Pine Island. A Mr. Sears lived at Water Lily on Currituck Sound and hired out to outfit, which meant he had skiffs and furnished guides. Unlike most of the Currituck folks, Mr. Sears raised and kept retrievers. His were the biggest, bulkiest, and best in the region, and they were all Chesapeakes. "Tougher 'n whitleather," Dad said.

About the end of the Season in 1908 or '09, Sears had a reservation for hunters from Philadelphia and persuaded Dad to stay and guide. When the hunters cancelled, Mr. Sears said he didn't have the money to pay Dad, but, "maybe you'll feel better if you take one of Sheila's pups." Now there was nothing an Atlantic Coast guide would rather have than one of the Sears's Chessies, so a bargain was struck.

In the litter was a gyp that stood out from the rest because, instead of the chocolate brown of the bitch and the dog, this little one was almost RED. Just about the color of a chow or redbone hound. She was first to come out of the box, and Dad promptly put the eight weeks-old youngster in the pocket of his hunting coat. And so, off south to Chester, and the girl Dad pined for—my mother to be. He named the pup "Rose," after mother, but nobody ever called her anything but "Red."

By the beginning of the following season she, with her inherited genes, weighed almost seventy pounds, and was destined at her peak (no pun intended) to tip the scales at well over a hundred. Dad said she was a natural retriever, having had a battering from an old crippled gander early on, and thereafter putting her foot on the head of every bird before picking up and returning. And she was the strongest swimmer in the community. Early on, because there were few retrievers locally, nobody knew just how much she was a mistress of the sea.

My Uncle Tom Fulcher, my mother's youngest brother, was just a boy when Dad brought Rose home. He was an old man when last I talked to him. Fulcher is a name well remembered in what are locally known as the "Straights Settlements," that series of fishing villages running north from the trading town of Beaufort, through Davis and Stacy and to Cedar Island, where a ferry ran to Portsmouth Island. Uncle Tom had operated the ferry and knew everybody within twenty miles.

I pressed him to tell me what he remembered about how things were, and especially about Rose that everybody called Red. Uncle Tom remembered that she would retrieve anything smaller than she was. Once there was a fire in the village, a residence belonging to some folks names Sawyer. He was the local butcher. The old house had withstood twenty hurricanes in its lifetime, but a careless hand with the kerosene heater spoiled that record in a trice.

Now in the days when there was no piped water and everyone relied on a dug well, there wasn't really much that could be done to quench a house fire. The crossroads had a "pumper" pulled by hand, and when a hose was tossed in a well, two volunteers pushed-pulled a rocking handle that forced water up from the well—at least until the well went dry. At the Sawyer's, twenty or so neighbors were rushing around and Uncle Tom and Zeke Mitchell were manning the pump, but throwing very little water. Then it was that Mrs. Sawyer began screaming, asking who had seen little Danny, her two year-old. She was fighting to go back into the burning house, holding the child's jacket which she had grabbed on her way to safety.

Uncle Tom said Dad came up about then and, sensing the peril the child might be in, snatched the child's clothing from the panicky mother and, sticking it under Red's nose, said "fetch." Now we aren't talking about bloodhounds, nor trained retrievers—just a young duck dog. Uncle Tom said he could have made the story really exciting if he had told me Red jumped through ten foot flames to make a rescue. The truth was, Red bored in under the smoke on the bedroom side of the house, found a retrievable that smelled like what Dad had been holding and, picking the youngster up by his britches, retrieved him to hand. Dad's hand, that is.

If nothing had, up until that time, made Red something special in the community, the saving of Danny Sawyer certainly did. Of course there was no medal, no reward, just a hug from Mrs. Sawyer and, next butchering, Mr. Sawyer dropped by Dad's with a shank bone.

Dad guided frequently when not registered as a surfman

or part-time surfman. Some of the people he'd guided for on Currituck followed him south, staying at Beaufort, or with boarding houses at Marshallberg, or Davis or a cross-road later named "Otway" for an ancestor of one of Dad's clients. Mr. Clarence Otway came from shipping in New York City, and frequently brought with him a fellow shipper, a Mr. Carter, and Otway's nephew, Andrew. Nobody locally would guide if Andrew was in the party because of his attitude, which to put on the best face, was simply "snotty." Once, however, when money was short, Mr. Otway asked Dad to make an exception and to take his party.

Dad said that he had access to a stilt blind in the sound, and finally agreed to take the three Northerners for the day. Shooting was good, and they were approaching the limits when Red brought in a canvasback and, shaking herself free of ice water, attempted to retrieve as always directly to Dad. Unfortunately, he told me, the dog had to bypass Andrew, who reached out for the bird. She would not drop. Whereupon, Andrew slapped her across the face. That was a mistake of the first order.

Now the first rule of guiding is restraint where paying clients are concerned, but Dad said he simply slapped the s--- out of Andrew, knocking him flat, and stood on his gun hand, still locked around the shotgun. Andrew got up shouting that he was getting a warrant for assault "as soon as I get to town." It was then that Mr. O, standing only about five feet six, quietly said to his kinsman, "That's enough, Andrew. Here's a hundred dollars for your return fare. We'll flag the launch to take you to Beaufort. I shall expect to find that you are on the four-o'clock train home." That story was to show me how Red stood in Dad's household.

And it was the same with the crews at the Life Saving Station, where she was adopted and pampered by all the crewmen. Which turned out to be a wondrous thing.

The winter of 1912-13 was rough on shipping off Beaufort Inlet, just south of Cape Lookout. On October 20th, in early morning, a steamship flying the "I am on fire" flag was spotted by one of the surfmen. The motor lifeboat was launched, and Dad and Red were part of the crew. Capt. Hart planned to beach his vessel, loaded with bales of cotton, ships stores and fruit. Mindful as always of the duty to save, if possible, not only passengers and crew but also cargo, Keeper Willis put his men to work fighting the fire which they did for sixty hours straight. All were saved in the case of the BERKSHIRE.

Dad would go on to tell me about the DORCHESTER, a steamer trying to salvage the ALCAZAR, which had been abandoned. And how, two days before Christmas, his crew started a pumping procedure that was to last into January. And about the THOMAS WINSMORE, a three-master, on which Dad and crew, with Red "assisting," hoisted anchors by hand and sailed into harbor.

But it was the wreck of the three-masted schooner, MANCHESTER HAYNES, on February 13, that makes this story. There was a SSW gale with very high seas. The captain could not clear the shoals, so anchored, but the deckload of yellow pine broke loose and she filled with water. The lifesaving crew was maneuvering to reach the disabled vessel, when the motor launch broached, throwing Red and six crewmen into the roaring surf. The Lookout shoals are sometimes shallow and sometimes deep. The winds from the SSW left some shoal water shallow enough so a man could stand—provided the undertow, or more properly the cross-currents, didn't sweep him out to sea. But between the shoals and the shore frequently lie deep sloughs. And humans wearing oilskins and sea boots, even if they kept their feet, had no hope of making land without help.

Somehow, my father said, Red seemed to sense the prospects, and the men's panic. She immediately swam to him and when he grabbed her collar, she headed straight northwest to shore. With that help, he fell flat on the sand, completely exhausted.

So he did not see, but only heard of, what happened next. Back went Red to her "boys" fighting to stay upright on the shoals. Three more times she ventured south into the wind to help a crewman back to safety. After four such rescues, the big, tough bitch would have tried again, but the last crewman, now on the beach, pulled her close. She never saw that two of the crew were no longer standing.

When Dad recovered enough strength to get upright, his first thought was for his dog. Down the beach he staggered until he came upon the survivors. Hugging Red to his chest, he wept for the lost members of the surfcrew. But those are the expected, those lost heroes of the Coast Guard. And for the Watermen and their dogs, life goes on.

Red continued to retrieve for Dad, and I, born two years later, remember her only as a tired old dog with a rusty coat and a grizzled muzzle. But on the little square in Chester there stands to this day a bronze marker, on which some sensitive sculptor of the Depression Federal Arts program has created a replica of a big Chesapeake looking out to sea. That's Red!

The Outlander

I t was just 'bout dark when I first saw him. I was takin' the yoke off Ring after ploughin' out the collard patch, and gettin' ready to put the hobbles on him so he could free-feed overnight up on the ridge. Ring was the ox that Paw had cut, oh, ten, twelve years ago when I was just a sprout. Maybe three or four. I was tendin' the garden 'cause Paw was away. He was pullin' time for 'shinin', makin' moonshine. We figgered he'd be gone quite a spell, 'cause this was his second time caught. Anyway, down in Atlanta he was at least eatin' good. That's more'n Ma and me and the little one was doin'. Things was tough everywhere, but 'specially in the hill country. Folks that had left to work in the little mills at Liecester and Canto were comin' home 'cause the Dee-pression had shut everythin' down. We'd had a pretty fair summer, what with the garden, blueberries, dandelion greens, and other stuff we could scrounge, but winter would be comin' on and I'd had a hard time pullin' enough fodder to last through for Ring and the old cow. We knew we'd have to keep the cow 'cause the baby needed milk, but Ring would have to go if the snow got so deep he couldn't forage.

Oh, about that man? He come down the spring path, so easy the hounds didn't even hear him. Wearin' a dark-colored suit, he was, not overhauls like most men-folks up here in the Blue Ridge. And his shoes was pretty dusty, but I could see they was almost new. His black hat was pulled down all around, and both arms was up, wrapped around a shotgun carried 'cross both shoulders, the way some folks rest when they've been huntin' all day. He shore didn't look like he meant no harm, but I reached for the pitchfork, just in case, 'lessen I hadn't read him right. Paw always said you never could tell what kind of outfit a revenooer would get himself up in, just to sneak up on a feller trying to make a dollar on lightnin'. "A man's got to feed his fam-'ly," Paw always said, and runnin' a still was 'bout the best way to do it. Ma'd been off to school, but Pa hadn't had much schoolin' and he said he could make more from corn in a jar then in the shuck. Well, he'd made his mistake, and now he was off an' gone, and I was the on-liest man left, and me with just a hay-fork.

Alongside the man was the damnedest-lookin' dawg I ever seen. It was short-haired and slick-tailed and speckled with a blue-tick, but almost white. But it shore warn't no hound. It ears was shorter, and it had a clean head with no dewlaps and somehow it didn't slouch around. It kept its head and tail up and looked sorta proud of itself.

Now, 'bout the time they stepped out of the laurel into our clearin', our two Plotts and the one Redbone come tearin' out from under the house, yellin' like all get out, and I just knowed that strange dawg was gonna get et up, else the stranger'd have to shoot mine. Them hounds ain't skeered of nuthin'. They'd take on anythin' from fox to deer to a sow bear with cubs. I started runnin' and hollerin', tryin' to cut 'em off before they got shot. That's when I first learned somethin' about that feller—he was tough! "Stay," he says to his dawg, real soft. "Now, *git!*" he says to mine, his voice as low and cold as if he'd been talkin' out of a well. And them three dawgs just stopped like they'd run into a hot-wire fence.

It was only then he swung the gun off his shoulders. He looks at me and says, "With that out of the way, I'll say howdy, and I need to talk to your mother."

Pa'd built us a pretty good house, bigger'n most in the cove. There was two rooms and the loft, and later he'd cut a door off the big room leadin' to a shed, all closed in. His brother, my Uncle Ed, was the best cabin builder, and still-maker, too, on our side of the mountain. With a pair of oxen, them two had wras-tled chestnut logs down the slope, notched, fitted, and chinked 'em, split whiteoak for a puncheon floor, and rived cedar shakes for the roof. "Just like Grandpaw built back in sixty-seven when he first come into this country," Uncle Ed said. They was lucky to find the chestnut, 'cause the blight had killed mighty near all those in the whole Blue Ridge. Course, our house did have glass windows, and there was even talk of the C.C.C. buildin' a power line in, but nuthin' come of it. Uncle Ed had made the mistake, down in Asheville, of drinkin' another man's likker, caught the jake-leg, and died right after Pa married Ma and moved into the new cabin.

Well, the hounds had gone back under the house, grumblin' and growlin'. Steppin' up on the stoop, the man pulled a tow-sack down off a nail, dropped it on the floor, and told his dawg, "Lie down." I never saw nuthin' like it, mine won't hardly come when I call 'em. Then, leanin' his gun against the door jamb, he reached underneath his coattails and pulled out three pa'trich from his belt and said, "Boy, I expect you'd better clean these for supper." Then he took off his hat, knocked on the door, told me to "scat," and I scatted!

When I come back from the wellhouse it was mighty nigh pitch dark, smoke was comin' out the chimney, and I didn't hear Ma screamin' or nuthin', but the door was shut and I was skeered to knock with that man in there. So I took the chance to look at the gun. It was double-barreled, but the barrels were some kinda short. The stock didn't have no pistol-grip; it was mighty purty grain, but so slim I didn't see why it hadn't broke. It didn't look real old, but it did have outside hammers, just like my old Grandpaw's 'cept much smaller. Alongside the rib I spelled out, "P-U-R-D-E-Y."

While I was heftin' the gun, which didn't weigh scarcely nuthin', old Nail, the Redbone, thought he'd take a chance on the man bein' out of sight to run off or chew up that *thing* layin' on *his* stoop. Backed by the Plotts, all mighty brave now, he come roarin' up the steps, ready for bear. The visitor jest coiled like a buggy spring, hit Nail with fang and shoulder, ploughed through both Plotts, rippin' as he went, and turned back on Nail, almost tearin' off an ear. Then he went back to chewin' up the other two. Before I could hardly put the gun down, the three home-dawgs had cut out for the timber, and the newcomer was standin' tall at the steps when his boss opened the door.

"Come in, boy," he said, not payin' much attention to the fightin' machine he'd brought with him 'cept to touch him betwixt the ears. Then, pickin' up the gun, he put a hand on my shoulder and took me inside.

Ma was sittin' on the hearth, rockin' the baby, and I could see she'd been cryin'. She reached out a hand and pulled me to her.

"This here's Mr. Lassiter," she says. "He's brought bad news." Then she broke out cryin' again. Mostly, Ma's mighty purty, what the mountain folks call a "comely woman," but now she looked terrible.

"You'll all call me Jim," the man says. "I've told your Mother"—he didn't say 'Ma'—"that your father won't be coming back. I'm sorry to have to tell you that he was killed in a knife fight in prison. The fight wasn't of his making. The truth is he intervened when a prisoner tried to cut me. You see, like your father, I'd made my mistakes, not moonshining, but a matter of bank funds. Let me get it all out so there'll be no secrets among us. The stockmarket crash left a lot of us bankers with loans unpaid and the banks going broke. Mine was one of them. The depositors demanded revenge. I had no wife or children, so I thought that if anyone in my bank had to go to prison, I'd better be the one. I never took a dime, but there I was, and some fellow, in jail for robbery, tried to work me over. Your father stepped between us. Before he died, I promised I'd try to help his family when I got out. So I went by home, picked up my things, my dog, and my gun, and here I am. I'd like to help out. The dog's name is Hi-Rolling Dan, but we just call him Dan. Now let's feed him and your stock, and eat our supper which your mother will be kind enough to fix. It'll help take her mind off her loss. I'll sleep in this shed over here tonight until I can make arrangements."

He wasn't Pa, but he shore was a kind man. Every day or so he'd walk up from Woodfin, down in the valley where he'd rented a room. Sometimes he'd bring Dan, and they'd go off together up in the laurel thickets and most always bring home some pa'trich, but he never took me with him when he hunted with Dan. He told me his dawg was a pointer, bred down from a line of great huntin' dawgs in England, that somewhere back there was a cross with a bull-dog or mastiff with fightin' blood. When Dan came, my dawgs left.

Other times him and me'd hunt rabbits and squirrels for the pot, me with old Grandpaw's long-barrel hammer-gun, and Jim with his little pop-gun. Once when we walked up a covey of quail, Jim killed two on the rise, dropped in another shell, and killed the sleeper. He was lightnin' with that Purdey-gun. I kept wonderin' why he never took Dan when him and me was huntin'.

Winter was late comin', and Jim kept helpin' out all that fall. He'd 'most always eat supper 'fore walkin' back down the hill. I thought maybe he was just lonesome, and a lot of time I'd leave him and Ma talkin' while I went to check the rabbit gums. Then one December afternoon, when me and Jim had just cellared the last of the cabbage and apples, a winter storm blew in from Tennessee. In ten minutes, the snow was blowin' through the cove, standin' straight out. The thermometer dropped twenty degrees. Jim was pullin' up his collar, fixin' to walk back to his place.

That's when Ma come out and says, "No, Jim, you'll stay with us. The children and I need you. The boy will sleep in the shed-room." Jim turned and put his arms around her, and we all went in to the fire. Sure 'nuf, I slept in the shed.

It was two weeks 'fore the preacher was due for services at the Woodfin Baptist Church. When he come that Sunday, Ma and Jim and me and the baby was waitin'. There was a marryin' after preachin'. Then all us fam'ly, includin' Dan, went back up the cove in a used Ford station wagon Jim had bought Ma for a weddin' present.

The next mornin' broke bright and sunny, but there was still four or five inches of snow on the roads, and the school busses wasn't running. That's when Jim come out after breakfast with a different look on his face. He looked plum serious, and I wondered if him and Ma had some problem. But it wasn't Ma, it was me lookin' at trouble. "First," he said, "I will not have an ignorant boy around here, murdering the King's english. I have therefore registered you for the next semester at the Asheville School for Boys. Next, today with no school is not too early for you to start learning to be a gentleman!" Then his whole face changed. He broke into a big grin, whistled up Dan, and says, "Son"—he really called me son—"let's go shoot us a mess of partridges." With that, he picked up Grandpaw's gun and handed *me* the Purdey.

The Ghosts of
Rosetree Plantation

he story of Rosetree Plantation and how it came to be haunted has been passed down in my family for the seven generations since the War Between the States. It is not a story exclusively within the family. Anyone living for any length of time in the rich bottom lands of the Chowan River in what North Carolinians call "Chowanoke" knows all about it. Of course, I never believed in ghosts. That is, not really. Except, maybe...?

Colonel Exree Robinson came home from the war with his empty right sleeve pinned. Home was the 6254-acre plantation his paternal ancestors had accumulated beginning with a thousand acres of land grant in times of the early Lords Proprietors. A great house overlooked the confluence of the two streams. It was furnished with English mahogany, Italian marble mantels, and French tapestry. It had escaped rape by Sherman's vandals who burned the courthouse at Winton, solely because Colonel Robinson's wife was herself a Yankee, with strong New England ties and impeccable Boston Brahmin heritage. And money.

The Colonel, however, was bitter about the loss of the war, the freeing of his slaves, the Northern foot upon the economic neck of the South, and his own disability. Especially that his passion for hunting was inhibited by the loss of his shooting arm. For before the conflict, he had spent much time and energy developing a kennel of pointing dogs intended to be the best in the South. He had managed to hold together the nucleus even after the surrender, and by the early 1870's had, with his wife's money, gone to England and there acquired the gem of all setter brood bitches. She was from the famous Laverback kennels, direct descendant of Laverback's Rhoebe, and The Colonel called her "Reba." Heavily ticked, dark like her granddame, she would today be called a blue Belton. She was all that he expected, throwing strong offspring with great noses and temperament. He even learned, but badly, to shoot lefthandedly when breech loading became available, using a sawed off smoothbore like a pistol.

Among the loyal former slaves working on the plantation was one Ishmael, in his early twenties, promoted from field hand to kennel man and helper to my great-great grandfather, who was Colonel Robinson's overseer. Now a freedman, Ishmael was given a cabin for himself and Cleone, his eighteen year-old wife, who had brought forth a child, a boy named Able, that was Ishmael's pride and love.

The tragedy began with a fire in the "quarters." Spreading rapidly, it had reached the roof of Ishmael's cabin, with Cleone overcome by smoke, but Able playing on the floor. Rushing into the smoke-filled room, Reba, who because of her status, ran loose, had caught the baby by its britches and was hauling him to safety. Then it was that the Colonel cracked. Seizing his prized dog by her collar, he dragged her free, only to leave the child and its mother to perish.

All this Ishmael saw as he ran from the barns three hundred yards away. In his hand, simply because he was hitching up a mule when the fire started, he carried a single-tree-hickory with forged iron rings at the ends. Fighting his way into the cabin, he saw his loss.

Seeing the Colonel now calling for the fire brigade, Ishmael simply stepped behind his employer, and brought down upon his head the implement at hand. The skull cracked like an egg. Coolly, going into the kitchen of the mansion, he picked up a side of bacon, a bag of meal, some matches, a butcher knife, and taking an axe from the wood-pile, disappeared into the swamp. It was said that the dog Reba went with him. At least she was never seen again.

The Colonel's wife simply closed the house after sending north two four-mule-team wagon-loads of household goods, and moved back to Boston. Some sort of trust held title to the property which went rapidly to wilderness. I must, to the lady's credit, say that she deeded a tract of a hundred acres to the overseer. It lay at the extreme eastern border of the plantation with about five hundred yards of creekbank. That's where I come into the picture, because all these generations later, the frame house built there is still "Grampa's," where we descendants have visited a succession of grandfathers, to this day.

The ghosts of the Colonel, Cleone, and Able took up residence at Rosetree. It is why the place was not vandalized. All the freedmen and their families left precipitously. Other locals kept their distance. It was said that on moonlight nights, Cleone walked wailing around the compound, looking for Able. And that the Colonel sat and cried for his behavior, great sobs being heard when the wind blew through the latticework on the mansion's porch. But scariest was the tale that Ishmael himself returned, carrying a bloody singletree, and followed by a long-haired dog that howled whenever he stopped walking.

Now, more than a hundred years later, I still visit my own grandfather, launching a canoe to fish for red-breasts in the creek and even venturing to invade adjoining Rosetree with a hunting buddy and our bird dogs. If we could fight our way to the interior, Preacher and I could hope for some good shooting. He really is a preacher, and a bird- hunting machine, although his dog, Judy, is a tailless Brittany. I'll say this, she's damned near as good as my three year-old pointer, Duke. Together, they work well, and we get more than our share of Bobwhite. We have never seen another hunter on the place.

I have gone a long way around to get to the happening that is the core of this story. In mid-December, Preach and I travelled from home the fifty miles east to reach Grandpa's, and from there into Rosetree. An unprecedented highway survey team had cut a sightline almost bisecting the eastern end of the old plantation, and near enough to the mansion to offer access, provided you'd fight briars as high as your head. We headed for the old garden site next to where the slave quarters had been, both dogs out front.

It was nearby that I saw something that made me call, "Preach, Judy is backing a strange dog!" Sure enough, Duke came up and sight-backed, and we walked in and killed three birds on the rise. Then we looked at the stranger. She had delivered one quail to hand, and started off in front of us. No one having called, whistled, or come up when we shot, we figured she, for it was a bitch, was simply lost. Taking advantage of this fortune, we worked through the morning with three dogs on the ground, as good as you'd expect to find anywhere.

Taking a break at noon, our visitor lay down as we sat. But on our taking out the sandwiches, I thought she was starving. I threw her a half, and she wolfed it down as though it had been a week since feeding. Certainly she looked pretty beat-up, but there was no question of her class and breeding. At day's end, she followed us to the truck, still lost. Putting out some dog-feed and a pan of water, I was able to get my hands on her. She was skin and bone. And no collar. So nothing to do but trick her into one side of the double dog-box, to take her home, advertise, and locate her owner. Certainly there was something strange about finding her where we did, with no close residences, no truck tracks, nothing to indicate where to take back this heavily ticked setter bitch that was such a hunter.

She didn't try to bite, so I slipped onto her neck one of my collars to facilitate controlling her when we got home. I didn't want her making a dash for it, and did want to put her in my pens, if only for overnight. The dog box on my truck I had copied from one built for my Cousin Herbert, an old bird hunter. Each side would hold three friendly dogs, or fighters could be separated. Our dogs had loaded into their usual left side. I didn't know enough about this lady to trust her with our dogs, so taking her by the collar, I led her inside, and carefully snap-locked the barred door to her now private compartment. She lay down on the straw as you would expect of a tired hunter. The tailgate stayed down because the box itself was secure.

It was late, and we didn't stop at Grandpa's, but headed straight home. I didn't drop off Preach as usual, because I might need some help with the new dog. It turned out that what I really needed him for was as a witness. Pulling into my driveway, I circled until I came up next to the dog runs, stopped the truck and went to kennel our load. THERE WAS NO DOG IN THE RIGHT-HAND BOX! The latch was tight on the closed door. Just, no passenger. I hollered for Preach, who was lingering in the cab from the cold. Together we racked our memories. starting at Rosetree, dog loaded, door closed, door latched, no intervening stops, And then remembered the story of Reba. Crazy, huh? Could the ghost of Ishmael have released his dog, and then RELATCHED THE DOOR! Of course not. No such things as ghosts! I'll swear that Baptist preacher made the sign of the cross. We never again found this jewel of a bird dog. And the preacher had to vouchsafe (a very old word for "verify") the facts. Nobody would have believed just me.

Ten days later I received in the mail a small package with a letter inside. The letter read, "Enclosed is your dog collar, which I found yesterday near Rosetree Plantation in Bertram County while running a survey line for the State. I also found the enclosed three fired shotgun shells."

Whether or not you are doubtful, the missive was signed "ISHMAEL P. ROBINSON. "

Author's note: Don't pooh-pooh the ghost theory. In WWII, all stateside aircraft accident reports came across my desk. One indicated that twelve members of a flight crew out of Norfolk took off on a navigation mission over water, but only eleven returned. Where did he go? Another related to a B-25 that, after the crew hit the silk, flew clear across the Gulf of Mexico before crashing on a mountain called El Viejo. Ghost pilot? And a crewless B-17 that landed on a Kansas prairie and possibly would be still taxiing had it not run out of gas. Who handled the controls? Last month I caught a coon in a big city-owned Have-a-Heart, his capture and lengthy incarceration evidenced by torn up turf in all directions. Once locked, it simply can't be opened from inside. But next morning—no coon! Either another coon or a ghost released him. You guess!

Sally

his is a story about a birddog, the man who owned him, and another man who was completely different. Hunting is, after all, a reflection of the men and dogs that participate.

We think in wonder about our dogs' memories. How did old Pat, Judge B.'s setter bitch, recall where she'd found every covey? Not just on home territory was she infallible, but if ever we hunted foreign soil a second time she seemed to have total recall, cantering straight from the truck to the nearest bevy she'd found on the prior trip. And how did Pete Foley's Bullet recognize him after being lost for four years? But most wonderful is how a dog, kept in a kennel all summer, knows that it's to ignore the scent of rabbit, deer, doves, and every other odor except that of quail for the rest of the season? But they do remember.

For years, Judge B. and I hunted in the Waxhaw

Creek area, near the North and South Carolina line. Sometimes we'd cross paths with other hunters, pass the time of day, whistle up the dogs, and hunt on. In all those years, somewhat remarkably, we never ran across a black birdhunter. Coonhunters, rabbithunters, deerhunters, but never a genuine shell-vested, pointer-dog hunter in ragged brierbritches like ourselves. It seems reasonable to suppose that the black hunters here in the South had a far greater need than ours for a tangible profit on the time spent hunting— that is, food on the table. So maybe they were just too smart to waste all that time for such little game as quail. That may be a sociological statement, but in any event it's true. Or was.

The Judge and I had for many seasons planted feed patches and posted about 2500 acres of Massey property under our bird-lease. It was not all contiguous. Sand-clay roads and the creek itself cut it into segments. By tradition and for identification, we gave names to these areas—the Crowe Farm, the Bottom Hunt, the Mobley Place, for example.

One afternoon at Mobley, close to its far border and near some bright new brick homes along a recently black-topped road, we roused a covey. Picking up a bird or two, we crossed the road after singles. There in a twenty-acre cutover milo field, we saw another hunter, duly attired and following two fine-looking pointers. They were solidly on point on one of "our" singles.

As the hunter turned from his dogs and came toward us, the difference in our skin-color was apparent. His dogs held. "I know you," he said. "You're Judge B. You have the Mobley Place posted. I don't hunt over there, but *this* is *my* territory."

Well, the Judge was not used to such direct and critical comment, and I saw the red begin to rise in his neck. But what had been said was reasonable—and persuasive. We called in our dogs and retreated.

The following spring, I was passing one of the new houses and the same hunter was in the yard, so I stopped and re-introduced myself, and asked his name. The incident of the fall was not mentioned. We had some friendly conversation about the scarcity of good birddogs, and I went on my way, remembering Robert Jones.

A season or two passed, and sometimes we'd see Jones and give a wave of the arm. Each side honored the road as a dividing line. Dogs come and go, and once in a while I'd notice Jones had a setter or two in addition, or substitution, for his pointers. I had refreshed my own kennel, acquiring a smart young white setter bitch from a farmer fifty miles away who advertised in the *Agricultural Review*.

I guess it was three years after I first met Jones that I happened to be hunting the Mobley territory alone, almost across from his house. He wasn't hunting that day, and he walked over. I thought he just wanted to see how a fellow hunter was doing, now that relations were friendly. I remember that he had to stop to let the newspaper delivery-man pass, stuffing papers into those black roadside boxes at every dwelling. When he finally came over, he said, unaggressively, "Mr. Henderson, I believe you've made a mistake."

Well, I bowed up a little because I was clearly on our lease. "What is it this time?" I asked, now expecting another confrontation.

By then my dogs were gathered in, nuzzling this stranger, and anxious to be off. "Sir," said Jones, "I believe you have my dog."

Now I was really hot! "*Your* dog, hell! What are you talking about?"

" 'Scuse me, but lemme explain. Late last year I was hunting down in Anson County. My white setter was picked up by a farmer in a red truck. I hollered, but he got away. Yours looks so much like my dog, I just had to check her out."

Still boiling mad, I said, "Robert, I don't want any trouble. I bought and paid for this dog, and if you think she's yours, just, by damn, identify her."

I knew she wasn't tattooed, and didn't have a mark on her, all white as she was.

"Sir, if you'll just bear with me a minute, I'd like to try a little experiment."

I whistled the dogs in. Leaning over *my* bitch, he spoke softly in her ear. "Sally, go fetch me my paper."

Trotting across the road and rearing up on his black box, that's exactly what she did.

Tales of Bird Dog Man

ery birdhunter, and certainly everybody who doubles as an outdoor writer, comes up with a story from time to time in which somebody else is the protagonist. So you seek to record the tale or tales against the day you're doing an article or writing a book. The late Harry Golden told me he kept these reminders in a whiskey barrel in his living room. Here are a couple I've saved, though not in a barrel, and though you don't know the dogs or their boss, you'll be glad I did.

The death of Colonel Frank Pierson at the Veterans' Administration hospital in Salisbury, North Carolina in early September 1993 marked, as we say, the end of an era. He was recognized with many medals for his army service, but my knowledge of the man was as a bird dog lover, trainer, breeder, and hunter. But not just bird dogs, as you shall see.

His obituary said that he was a member of the American

Field Hall of Fame, which may have overstated the case. If not, he should have been. He spun lots of yarns around the field trial circuits from coast to coast, and dog men have repeated them. But, to the best of my knowledge, these two have had no national exposure. I think you dog lovers deserve, through these stories, to know the man.

Late in the 1950's, I was hunting quail pretty regularly with a fellow named Cecil Steele down in Union County, North Carolina. Cecil kept dogs of his own and also boarded for others. Among the boarders one year was a small tri-color setter bitch. I owned and hunted a mirror-match in my Rebel's Polly Who?, the two being so nearly identical that I could barely tell my own dog. Both were top-flight performers, far better than average. Polly had already won some first place silver in field trials, and the other dog was equally good, though I hated to admit it.

Cecil said the visitor belonged to a Colonel Pierson, whom I had met at a field trial or two. He was memorable for his continuing to wear a Smokey-bear hat and WWI puttees in lieu of bird boots. He wasn't hunting that year, which was his loss. Thinking he might not know the true value of his treasure, I schemed to buy her at the end of the season, but when I went back to Cecil's, he told me Pierson had sold her for a thousand dollars.

You probably could have bought a young Warhoop Jake or Sports Peerless for that price in the mid 1950's. I was astounded, and the next time I saw the Colonel I confessed my covetousness and inquired about the dog. "Well," he said, "I'll tell you a story."

"I was going to a little field trial in late February at Hoffman (the big-time tournament site near Pinehurst). I took the little dog I called Sue to enter in the All-Age. Oh, I knew she was that good! It snowed and no one else showed up. I was alone at the clubhouse and making the most of it. The first day, I had hunted Sue for at least one limit." He smiled. "A big limousine driven by a chauffeur pulled up. In the back was a middle-aged man and— ahem—a rather younger lady. He dismounted in the snow, saw my birds lying out on a table, and wanted to know, 'Is that your dog?' and 'Did she find those birds?' Then 'Is she for sale?' I quickly answered yes, yes, and a big No. No sale, no price!

"The upshot was that he identified himself as a Mr. Mars who made candy, and that he would like to rent Sue for the final week of the season at his south Carolina plantation, where the season had another week to go. I thought his credit was good, so I let him take her. She left, cuddled in the lap of the unintroduced lady passenger.

"Three days into the week, Western Union called to say I had a message and a money order. The message was 'I bought Sue.' The money order was for an unbelievable one thousand dollars. I cashed it!"

On another occasion, some years later, by chance also at Hoffman, where the big dogs run, I again bumped into the Colonel. I remember that dog prices had really exploded since Sue's day, because the two Flatwood dogs had just brought a reported $40,000. The Colonel was leaving his parked car, and I noticed a sort of off-breed feisty dog left behind. "Colonel," I inquired, (I always used the respectful title), "you have just reported two dogs as sold to the Japanese at what's about ten grand each. Why do you have such a mutt for your personal dog?"

Once more he said "I'll tell you a story." And this is what he told me:

"Not so long ago, in early Fall, I was leaving Jet— that's the mutt—in the car. Two fellows noted to me that I had left my brake lights on. I looked around, and sure enough, the red lights were on. so I thought a minute, and then I said 'Thanks, I'll have my dog Jet turn them off.' So I whistled through my teeth, and the lights went off, and Jet's head appeared through the back window. You can believe there was some real amazement on the faces of those two guys.

"What they didn't know was that on hot days in the early part of the field trial season, Jet would crawl under the dash to get in the shade. When he did, he leaned on the brake pedal, turning on the red lights. When I whistled, Jet jumped up, releasing the pedal, and the lights went out. Simple as that!" He gave me a wicked little grin.

The Colonel being probably now running Sue at some Hoffman-in-the-sky, and no longer hereabouts to tell his own tales, I thought I'd do it for him.

The Witness

t was just an ordinary lookin' dog, 'bout meejum size, hair not long, not short; tail not slick, not bushy; muzzle sorta keen, but right square head. Frank first noticed it—her—him? (a question settled at the first fire hydrant) as he was walking home from the shopping center. Mamie had sent him for some two percent milk. "We both," she said, "need to take off weight." Which was unhappily true, so he had walked, arthritic knee and all, the six blocks after supper.

They didn't eat "dinner" at his house. Dinner used to be at noontime when he was a boy, and all the black farm hands brought in their teams and "took out" in the barn lot back of Frank's daddy's big white house. Daddy would leave his law office to come home for old-bacon ham, boiled new potatoes, string beans cooked with the ham hock, squash fried in bacon drippings, cornbread *and* hot biscuits. And he would drink down a quart of real milk, three inches of cream at the top of the bottle shaken in before pouring. "None of that hy-moj-e-nation," thought Frank. "Those were the good days, before the Dee-pression." Days when he had been sent off to prep school, then the state university, flying high with his own Model A convertible, girls in his bed and money in his pocket. He'd done well only in English Lit and History. No matter, though, because after they'd lost the farm, he went to clerk at the hardware, and, somehow stayed for forty years. There, the vernacular of the carpenters, farmers, and fix-it men had supplanted the impeccable grammar his mother had insisted upon. Now the kids were grown and gone, and there wasn't much to talk about at home. Mostly at night he just read.

About the second block toward home, he turned and shushed the dog. At the back door, though, his companion was still there. "Well," the man said, "I might as well get a look at you. C'mere, dawg!" Under the porch light, a bit reserved, the visitor presented himself. "M-mm, reasonably clean, no ticks in the ears, probably some fleas. Those ribs look like you could do with a meal." A faint tail wag noted acceptance of the analysis. The absence of a collar assuaged the slight guilt Frank might have felt about feeding another fellow's dog.

Both tippy-toed through the back porch, the newcomer seeming to sense the need for stealth. Quietly putting the milk in the ice-box (Frank always called it "ice-box," even after they bought the Frigidaire with the tower on top), the host rummaged through the left-overs, found a bowl, dumped in the vegetables, a hunk of meatloaf, and a couple of slices of stale bread, and poured a pint of the two percent. Dog seemed to think it was a banquet.

About the time the meal disappeared, around the corner came 'Stopheles the cat. A feline squall brought Mamie in a hurry. Frank knew the roof was about to fall in. But the dog, with remarkable aplomb, not only didn't chase the cat—he walked over, sat down, and extended his right paw to Mamie. Now, even a surprised and angry housewife isn't going to take a broom to a *polite* dog. So they named him Buck, and Buck stayed. Although the couple had the cat, it was still sorta lonesome with all the kids off yonder out of touch. Eventually, even 'Stopheles seemed glad of company.

A few weeks later, Mamie announced she was attending the D.A.R. Armistice Day "readings," an all-day affair. The store being closed, her husband determined to take himself to the old home place to fish the back pond. The owners, who had bought the farm at foreclosure, rented out the house and the front hundred acres to sharecroppers. Posted signs were everywhere.

When he opened the door to the battered pickup, Buck was in like a flash. "Wot-n-hell," said Frank, "am I goin' do with a dawg—fishin'?" But he eased his stiff leg in and headed "home." "Home, hell," he thought. "Life ain't been too sweet. Gettin' to be an old man, fishin' buddies about all dead, and damn sharecroppers livin' in the Big House. And I have to sneak in to fish in my own pond. I'm gonna get d-r-u-n-k, and enjoy my misery." When he stopped at a cabin known to purvey a little store-bought likker on dry holidays, Buck seemed to nod approval.

In the country, after dampening his palate, he took from the gun rack a little .22, plinked for a while at cans and bottles at the roadside, and cussed the vandals who'd besmirched his landscape. Disgusted, he and the dog wandered down to the pond.

There, leaning back against the bole of a blackgum, the old man reopened his fifth of Heaven Hill, adequately irrigated his tonsils, and flipped in line, bobber, sinker, and red worm. Then he sat back to satiate himself with his self-pity. Buck sat, watching the float. An hour later, mellower by far, the man was fantasizing about how, if things had been different, he'd be living "up there," scion of aristocracy, lord of the manor, rich beyond dreams. He would have a BMW, fine wines, travel—travel maybe to to Spain, to Alaska. He hummed a snatch from "Valencia," then lapsed into a slurred recitation of "a-bunch-of-the-boys-were-whooping-it-up-in-the-Malemute-Saloon."

Frank, now well oiled, suddenly thought he heard a voice. It seemed to come from some dog, an apparition there beside him.

Voice: Bunch of the boys, huh? You ever been to Alaska? Reminds me of one of my forebears, also name of Buck. You must have had some precognition, using one of my more erudite words, in giving me the same cognomen. That Buck was pretty much royalty, a hero in a book by that fellow London. Jack, I think his name was. Buck was a great in-fighter; made his name trouncing some bulldog type, using the dash and slash technique.

Frank: Forebears? Ancestors? I'll have you know my father was Blackjack Pershing's aide-de-camp in World War I.

Voice: And mine, Sir, on the dachshund side, was Hitler's wardog. The family weren't too proud. Both had uncontrollable flatulence and were never welcome at family reunions.

Frank (showing growing annoyance): My grandfather fought with Lee before Richmond.

Voice: Mine was a Plott from Graham County—now there's a bit of ancestry for you. Couldn't keep his paws off a blue-tick bitch, though, and Grandma, who was a registered redbone, got sore as hell!

Frank (shrill, cutting in): Now, see here. My folks came from Scotland, where they were a sept of the clan MacDonald. That ought to stop you!

Voice: Scotland? I, too, have in m' bones a wee drap o' Scotch blud. I'm descended from Bob, whose father was named Battle, and the exploits of *my* clan were recorded for posterity by one Oliphant. See if y' kin top that!

Frank (befuddled): Well, well—damn! I'm being put down by a dawg, a bite-the-hand dawg.

Voice: Also, my line stems from a fighting French poodle who came over with William of Orange and whipped the English in the Battle of Hastings. So you see I, myself, am the quintessential synthesis of all great dogs. I bear the blood of Lassie, my great-aunt once removed; Rin-tin-tin, mogul of the movies, was my uncle. I am poodle-hound-shepherd-setter, the *nonpareil;* I am—"

(*BAM!* A single shot.)

Frank (suddenly sober): "My gosh, here I've got the story of a lifetime to tell the guys at the store—and I've *gone and killed the only witness!*"

Trouble on Currituck

here had been trouble at the high school that afternoon—another fight between Joe Sawyer and Jack Outlaw. Principal Midgette, who had been in the county school system for almost forty years, had sighed, knowing he'd soon have to take a hand. The boys came by it naturally, what with three generations on both sides always clawing at each other. But these two were getting too big and strong, and somebody was going to get seriously hurt.

This thing between the families was said to have started back in the thirties. Depression times, and cash money hard to come by down on Currituck. The market hunters were long gone, but with no money for children's shoes or even a bag of cornmeal, almost every man-jack from Water Lily to Kitty Hawk Bay and probably all along the coast picked up a few bucks peddling a pair of canvasbacks or a dozen sprig for whatever they could get at Elizabeth City or even Norfolk where a law-blind trucker was running north. Paradoxically, Jack Outlaw's grandfather, Sam, had been a game protector, straight and super-tough. The Sawyers had always made their living from the water—fishing, guiding, or with the Coast Guard. They were proud of their standing in the community, and justifiably so.

Only two people really knew what had happened back in the marsh that December night in thirty-four. Well, actually, three people, but that didn't come out until much, much later. Protector Outlaw had seen a light near an airhole where no light was supposed to be. On instinct and a lot of local knowledge, in pitch dark, he'd stumped a quarter-mile west from the highway, the big Redball hipsters slipping and sliding from hummock to hummock in the frozen marsh. Halfway there, three shots had rung out. At the edge of the water, he heard splashing off to the south, out of range of his flashlight. In the reeds, he found three black ducks, still warm. He also found Bill Sawyer's knit watchcap. Only Billy, whose wife had knitted it, wore a cap with a green tassel. He'd have been kidded off the Sound, except that he was too big to fight and too good-humored to laugh at. Billy would just laugh with you.

Next day, Outlaw "picked him up and took him in," as enforcement folks put it. It was the only case the officer lost that season. "Insufficient evidence," ruled the magistrate.

After that, the families didn't get along too well. There wasn't any real feud, not anything like that Mc-

Coy thing folks were singing about on the radio. Just a stand-offishness, punctuated by a scuffle or two among the youngsters. Neither Sam nor Billy would talk about it. Still speaking a bit like their English fore-bears, people living along the Outer Banks and the inland sounds of the Carolina coast don't talk much anyhow.

But in the current generation, there seemed to be more heat. Those two, fighting just before the school bus left, really seemed to hate each other. The pretty little Barco girl couldn't seem to make up her mind between them and obviously enjoyed her indecision. And the two young huskies had both wanted to quarterback the Blue Wave. Sawyer won out, and was understandably a bit cocky about it. Outlaw had elected to spend fall afternoons working a fishing boat and breaking a retriever.

You need to know about the dog. Back in April, Jack had stopped in one afternoon to see one of the Sears boys over at Water Lily. The Searses had always raised Chesapeakes—big, bold, mean and tough. They were some of the first on the Sound to use water dogs. Most guides had simply poled their juniper skiffs after crips, but Labs and goldens had begun to show up with the professionals in the fifties. However, a Sears-line-bred Chessie was something to behold, and getting one out of the family was, to a guide or would-be guide, netting the Holy Grail. Jack wanted, more than anything (even Sallie Barco) to get his guiding license.

So it was that he "just dropped by" some afternoons about the time a deep-chocolate bitch named Lily was about to drop a litter. He was a couple of weeks late, though, and when he looked through the penwire, a deep growl from the old lady pushed him back—but not before he saw, over the edge of the litter box, a pair of M&M eyes just beginning to open. "By gosh," he thought, "he's peeking at me." He chuckled at the unexpected pun. As to the pup, Jack had an inside track. He'd hauled in the senior Sears when that gentleman was caught out of gas one cold February afternoon, and there'd been a sort of half-promise of a pup "some time I don't have 'em all sold."

Luck had been with the boy, and a month later he'd walked away carrying Peek in his slicker pocket. Well, hell, everybody else called their dogs "Ches" or "Chester" or, with females, always "Chessie."

Peek was true to the promise of his huge feet. And his heritage. He was going to be one monster of a retriever. That summer, during his lanky stage, the boy worked him at every opportunity. Yard breaking wasn't too hard. By September, Peek weighed seventy-five pounds, swam like a rockfish, and chased every summer duck and coot in sight. He was retrieving block dummies cut from yellow poplar—when he could see them thrown. He was the figurehead on Jack's skiff all summer, a familiar dark silhouette against the rose of dawn and the copper of sunset. Jack tethered yard ducks in the Sound or threw dead domestics, and the big yearling Chesapeake was impeccable in bringing back the game.

But *only* when he marked it down. The stubbornness of the breed showed up whenever Jack tried to work him with hand signals. Peek simply would not take directions. Consequently, he thrashed around all over the place, searching when Jack threw a blind double, and while that constant activity may have strengthened his swimming muscles and improved his wind, it did nothing to increase his boss's confidence in what would happen in a blind.

There had been little improvement when Peek, now close to a hundred pounds, opened his first season. The problem was unresolved. Consequently, Jack hunted alone, unwilling to expose his failure to bring the pup around. Pride runs strongly in young men who want to become Currituck guides.

It was late on a December afternoon, a twenty-knot northeaster at his back, the eighty-horse Mercury pushing the heavy skiff and with Peek standing ice-covered, that Jack was running back to the mainland. The barometer was down and dropping. The boy had crossed the Sound to pick up his blocks from the blind he held off the Gun Club marsh. A pair of bluebills sitting in the lee of the blind made the fatal mistake of flushing back over the boat, and were scooped up on the fly. No hunting the morrow. The Corolla lighthouse, aft, was already blocked from view by the blowing spin-drift. It would be a nasty night.

Swinging wide of the weedbeds he knew so well, and off the village of Grandy where the lights were starting to come on, Jack suddenly was aware of a darker shadow off his port bow. At a hundred yards, even with the chop the wind had kicked up on that shallow body of water, it was apparent that somebody's boat had capsized. It had gone aground in shoal water, too shallow for the boy to run alongside.

Beyond, sitting up in the shallow water, was Joe Sawyer, obviously exhausted and possibly in shock. You don't let personal dislikes interfere when another waterman is in danger or hurt—not in a close community. So Jack hollered, "Walk on out, man, so I can pick you up."

But Joe, trumpeting his hands, shouted, "Can't walk—think I broke my heel."

It was too late to run for help, and the wind was building up. Hypothermia would get Joe in another half-hour. Spinning the wheel and standing off upwind, Jack fastened a line on Peek's collar, then heaved one of the bluebills as far toward the other boy as he could. His hope—a slim hope—was that the dog, retrieving, might get close enough to let Joe grab the line. But the wind had pushed the waves into whitecaps and the Chesapeake obviously couldn't keep a sightline on the dead duck.

Knowing it was futile, the young owner, now double-anchored, once more tried to work the dog toward Joe. Frantically signaling, "back, back," then swinging his left arm to the right, Joe suddenly saw a miracle. Peek was actually looking back at him each time he crested a wave and, for the first time, following orders. It seemed a lifetime, but in four or five minutes the big, rugged waterbuster honed in on his prize, now held by the injured young man. Joe couldn't hold onto the duck, but he did grasp the line and, shortly, Jack heaved Peek and the duck over the stern, then reversed and pulled Joe off the bank and into waist-deep water where he, too, was dragged aboard.

A couple of weeks later, the Christmas oyster-roast was underway in the high-school gym. Gathered there were Whitsons, Davises, Midgettes, Searses, Swanzeks, yes, and Barcoses, Sawyers, and Outlaws, all the old family names and a few new ones. Joe, wearing a cast, and Jack sat together on an overturned fishbox. Sallie Barco, glowing like a Christmas candle, was gazing into the eyes of the basketball center.

Principal Midgette walked up on stage, banged a cooking spoon on a tin tray, and held up his hand. "Folks," he said, "this is for all of you. I'll be retiring in the spring, after forty years. But what I've got to tell goes back even further—back to a December night in the mid-thirties.

"I have carried a pain in my heart all this time for what hurt this community and, especially, two families. That night, Pop was off with the surfboat, trying to save the 'Sallie Sue,' aground off Duck. Ma and the girls were hungry. We didn't have a dime at the house. I went to the store to try for credit, but I was too proud to ask. It had begun to snow, and I didn't even have a hat. Billy Sawyer was there. He pushed his knit hat with the green tassel over my ears and said, 'Get on home, boy.'

"I had three shells in my pocket. I'm the one that killed the three ducks and ran when Mr. Outlaw almost caught me. I hope I would have confessed rather than let Billy do time, but he came clear and it was just easier to keep my mouth shut.

"I'm sorry, I'm really sorry. But there it is."

Tears glistened on the old man's cheeks. As a matter of fact, tears flowed everywhere. Joe and Jack looked at each other, got up, and lifted the principal to their shoulders. Then the rest of his students, even the basketball center, joined in and carried him offstage—just like a winning coach.

Postscript: Despite the use of certain names and places, all of this story is fictional, and no real person, living or dead, is represented herein. As to the Sound, I love the place and the people.

Cap'n and Miss Ellie

llie Olson was thirty four years old when IT happened! She had been the librarian in Popple City, Minnesota, since being graduated from the State Normal School for Teachers. A dozen years later, some sort of flu-like virus took her down for almost a month. At the end of that time she could not speak. She took a leave of absence and learned sign-speak, but mostly she wrote on a pad that was her constant companion.

There must be dozens of "Popples" located from Colorado to the Canadian border (and past that, for all I know.) Hers had about fifteen hundred permanent residents, escalating to thrice that in summer when visitors came to try for lake trout, and, of course smelt in season. The adjacent body of water, Lake Sorrow, was about a thousand acres in size, and was ordinarily misnamed, being a very happy vacation spot and not too bad in winter, what with the ice fishing and ice-boating.

The citizens loved their librarian, and pooled funds to buy for her, when she returned, a two year-old black Labrador bitch that had been trained to observe and obey hand-signals. An opposite number for the famed seeing eye dogs for the sight-impaired. Her mistress, being a lively lady unwilling to withdraw from life, although a bit shy with strangers, thoroughly enjoyed "working" Gretta. Almost every day, before or after work as the light allowed, the two played outside Ellie's snug little house, the dog gradually becoming a near-genius at understanding her boss, and quickly going through the sit/stay, heel, and other yardbreaking. Unexplainably, however, Gretta simply would not "fetch." Unlike almost any known Lab, although she would carry a coke-bottle around, she seemed to have no interest in throw-and-retrieve.

Aside from the dog, Miss Ellie, as the community had come to call her, seemed to have many acquaintances, but few friends. She was about five foot six, maybe a hundred twenty pounds, well distributed, and had a beautiful complexion. It was her smile, though, that seemed to light up the library whenever someone she knew came in to pass the day, or especially when she could find a special book for an inquiring child. She lived alone, her parents having died some years before. It was from them she had inherited the house, and that probably was what kept her in Popple City. Should she have had a boy-friend, the whole town would have known it in twenty four hours. It was that kind of small town.

So that was the situation in June, two years after her affliction struck. There appeared at the library one afternoon, a stranger to the town. He identified himself as

Harry Barker, captain, USN, Ret. He told Miss Ellie that he had been born in the County, but had gone away to the Academy when he was eighteen, and having had a bit of an accident on active duty, had been kicked up a rank by his buddies from Annapolis as was customary, and had elected to come back "home." Such was more than he ordinarily would have talked, but the women behind the desk was so obviously attractive, his tongue simply got away.

She in turn, blushed a bit, and, by her notepad, inquired what she could get for him from her shelves. A man of some aplomb, he showed no flicker of curiosity, and continued what rapidly became a two-way communication, albeit with only one vocal. Gretta being at her place under the desk, came out to see what was going on. And the Cap'n, warming to the new acquaintenceship, hastened to scratch under her chin and rub up her ears, much to that girl's delight. "Mam," he said, "what a coincidence. My side-kick these days is Admiral, also a black Lab, and of impeccable breeding, which obviously is true of—what was her name? Gretta." This blond six footer with the engaging grin and the strange walk, though retired, could be no more, she thought than fifty. What was the mystery he seemed to carry with him?

It was not long, then, until Popple City had something to talk about! The Cap'n was at the library every day. He couldn't be reading all those books. By George, the man had his eye on our Ellie. As for the two principals, it seemed natural enough to first go to a picture show, then to church, and sometimes his Chevy was parked outside her house until—well, never really scandalously late.

Each had disclosed schooling, favorite tunes, special tastes in food and drink (but not too much of the latter). The Cap'n had even told how he acquired the limp that led to his early discharge. It seems he was transferring from a tender to a destroyer, when the vessels clashed, crushing his right foot, which was now a remarkable piece of machinery. But not quite perfect. Sometimes it went port when he commanded starboard.

At some point, the two dogs would have to meet. That they seemed favorably inclined toward each other, the big male and the diffident lady-dog, simply made it easier on the couple to attend to human affairs. Came the time, though, when a lady's magazine would say "love struck." This being a publication a bit more realistic, you will recognize an awkward moment when the Cap'n observed to Miss Ellie, "Admiral has become aware that Gretta will soon be 'in the mood for love,' as he quaintly put it. "It's simply too embarrassing for me to discuss" she wrote. "Why don't you take over and do whatever is customary to, to, to accommodate them." And so the Cap'n and Admiral invited Gretta to their quarters and the deed was done.

A couple of days later, Admiral, jumping out of the back of the Cap'n's pickup, pulled a large muscle in his left hind leg. The good Doctor Baron, who was the local vet, devised a large cast from hip to foot, and thus the big dog was grounded and could not attend the Sunday sail that, in early summer, had become a weekly occurrence with the couple and their two Labs.

On this particular Sunday, Lake Sorrow could have looked no happier. The sky was that cerulean blue that made white cumulus even whiter. The breeze was at eight knots. Strangely, there were relatively few boats out. The Cap'n's ketch-rigged sixteen foot skiff was bouncing joyously, when a sudden front closed in quite quickly. They were half a mile off shore and coming about when a gust swung the boom visciously, catching the Cap'n across his shoulders, his bad foot twisted, and over he went. Fortunately, he was down wind of the craft, and all would have been well with a powerful swimmer like Harry, but he was seized with a terrific cramp in his injured shoulder.

The swinging boom had fouled the rigging, and Ellie knew she could not handle the boat and make a rescue. Suddenly she grabbed Gretta's muzzle, pushed in a float-bumper with line attached, and—

Suddenly she heard herself screaming "Go! Go! Gretta." And miraculously Gretta WENT. Over the taffrail carrying the float-bumber, straight to the Cap'n, who was calling "fetch." Safely back on deck a few moments later, he found himself locked by Ellie in the warmest of embraces. He took only a second to mutter a "Well Done" to Gretta, and then devoted himself vigorously to returning the affection.

The whole scenario had been seen from the beach, and the welcome half hour later rivaled a New York heroes' parade. In a smaller version, of course. Strangely, it did not seem anti-climactic when Ellie, from the dock, told the crowd, in a voice that ALL COULD HEAR, "Last week Gretta got her man, and by golly, I wasn't going to lose mine!"

Goosey, Goosey, Gander

trictly speaking, this isn't a "dog story," because the dog involved got badly upstaged by events as they occurred. But he was present and on board, and at least a witness. If there was a deficiency in his guard dog chores, it was not of the spirit, which was great, but of the flesh, which had weakened with age. For he was 12 dog-years, the equivalent of 84 in human count, the same age as his mistress. And this writer, which may be why he got into this story at all.

A dozen years before, the late Ed Gaskin had retrieved him, an abandoned and hungry puppy, from a roadside wandering and brought him home to his wife, Emma. By appearance, the pup was part retriever, but the couple affectionately called him "Mutt." He grew to a passable working dog for a duck guide because he loved to retrieve, but mostly he was just company for Emma when Ed was away. After Ed's passing the bond between widow and dog grew tighter. He would bark at strangers, but had never bitten anybody.

No one would have suspected that she lived in fear. Outwardly, Emma Gasskin was bright, cheerful even what her neighbors would call "fiesty." Emma was now a widow, eighty-four years old, and she lived as she had for fifty years, there in the little frame house with the picket fence, backed up to the black-water creek where Ed used to dock his thirty-foot Islander and eighteen foot juniper skiff.

The little settlement was called Davis Landing (or it could have been called Oriental, or Vandemere, or Cedar Point—any of which would have served this story, for all the inhabitants for two hundred years had made their living from the water.) The brackish creek ran through the marshland, meandering into Core Sound which, in turn, offered openings into the Atlantic off the North Carolina coast. In the early eighteenth century the inland waterways, protected from the ocean's fury by the redoubtable Core Banks, were said to have been the lairs of pirates like Blackbeard and Anne Bonney. Now there was a tough dame who'd swing her saber and decapitate a sailor like slicing a cabbage.

Emma had read of her, and some nights she wished— well, a saber wouldn't be a weapon of choice because her hands were all knotted up with arthritis, and she couldn't even hoe her bit of garden. Mutt was about as bad, gimpy in the shoulders, and slow in getting up from his sleeping sack at the back door.

With all the traipsing up and down the creek, boats running without lights, something bad was going on. The

Morehead City newspaper kept talking about drugs, and now that Florida was being patrolled so heavily, the drug runners had moved up to the Carolinas. There certainly was no more likely territory, what with all the marsh, and creeks and rivers. But to get in from the ocean, only an expert boatman could manage, which meant that one or more of her neighbors were involved.

Emma was shrewd enough to know that if she were believed to recognize them "at work," her house might be burned, or even her throat cut. It was horrible to think who might have been caught up in such traffic. Could it be true of Sam Fulcher, or Johnny Chalk, or one of the Davis boys, all of whom kept her wood cut and her garden cultivated? Yet she knew the terrible red tide had this summer invaded these Carolina waters from the south. Shellfishing for clams and oysters was banned, shrimp were suspect. The market was wiped out, and those boys had babies to feed and mortgages to meet. Who knows the ways of temptation?

But Emma refused to dwell on the unpleasant. There had been, and still were, good days—great days, even. She had come to the straights-settlements half a century before to teach at the local grammar school. Young Ed Gaskin, fisherman, oysterman, and duck/goose guide, had spotted her the first Sunday at the Methodist Church. Halfway through the service, his deep blue eyes had locked into her amber ones and, she mused, had never let go. She had taught for a while, lost their only child, kept house for Ed for forty years, watched him tool the skiff or little Harkers Island off-shore boat in and out of the creek. He went, in good weather and bad, bringing back oysters, fish, eels, or strings of ducks and geese as the seasons dictated. Sometimes with nothing at all. But love, that is—always coming back with love. Then, ten years ago, he was gone.

Since then, she had puttered about, keeping her house as best she could. She still went to church on most Sundays, and once a year, at the end of term, she was recognized at the graduation ceremonies at the school. The arthritis kept creeping up, stiffening her knees and hips, but the hands were the worst, the knuckles sore and swollen.

She had great empathy with Mutt, who hobbled along behind her on trips to the garden. She kept hoping, ever optimistic, that research would develop a cure. She knew that dogs were involved in experiments. Maybe there would be some relief for the next generations, man and dog.

Then one spring day, something happened that really gave her spirits a lift. She was out feeding corn to her few chickens when she sensed, rather than saw, a pair of Canada geese light on the creek. Later that week she was delighted that they had waddled up on the bank and were feeding with her biddies. Canadas, she thought, ought to be off and gone to the far North. This pair had apparently been short-stopped. Maybe one or the other had been hurt during hunting season and couldn't make the long flight. Whatever she'd never know, but she couldn't have been happier when she spotted a nest in the edge of the marsh just beyond her lilac bush near the path to the unused landing.

Emma wasn't much for giving people-names to animals. She just thought of them as "Goose" and "Gander." But she put out extra corn at nightfall, and next morning it was gone. With her binoculars she spent hours that first week watching the parents alternating on the nest, one sitting, the other feeding or keeping lookout. Mutt's curiosity had come to a quick end when the gander hissed him.

It was in the second week of the housekeeping that *it* happened. Glassing the area late one afternoon, Emma saw two power boats pulled up, bow to stern, on the far side of the creek. Something, in small bags, was being passed from one to the other. In one she recognized Bobbie Davis. The skipper of the other was a stranger, swarthy and bearded. Certainly not one of the locals. Then there was a shout! The setting sun must have reflected off her lenses because both men jumped to the consoles. Bobby headed off downstream, wide open. The stranger headed straight for Ed's landing. Emma, who was standing in her backyard, turned and started for the house. The old knees would not be hurried. Glancing over her shoulder, she saw the man drawing a sheath knife as he heeded in her direction.

Now that fellow may have known drug running but he didn't know geese. No sooner had he set his feet on the path than he was met by two black, grey and white destroyers. Necks outstretched, hissing like a pair of overheated boilers, wings akimbo, hurtling to the attack. Goose, as they say in football, took him low. Gander went for the head. In a second, the man was on his back, knife lost somewhere in the marsh. Goose, her head powered by a pikledriver neck, seemed to be bent on destroying his masculinity with a four pound hammer. Gander, with wing butts like war clubs, sought to join his ears by driving them through his skull.

When finally freed from the hospitality of the nesting

geese, the bearded man stumbled toward the house. But that was a dubious haven. Old Mutt, graying muzzle and all, took over. Charging the stranger's left flank, Mutt sank his well-worn canines in the region of the hip pocket swinging there like a black and brown caboose.

"Call him off," the man hollered. For there, standing on the stoop, was the tiny gray-haired owner, pointing at his belt-buckle what seemed to be a very, very large shotgun. From the small figure came a surprisingly firm voice. "Down, Mutt." she said. And then, "Sir, you are contemplating the business end of Ed Gaskins' 12-gauge loaded, despite the difficulty it caused me, with number two buckshot. My hands are crippled with arthritis, but I assure you, sir, I can still bend the trigger finger. Now march! Into that closet facing the wall." The key clicked.

A moment later, by phone, "Is this the Sheriff's office? Billy? This is Emma Gaskins. Come on out. A pair of geese and ole Mutt have a present for you. No, Billy, I haven't lost my mind. But I may have found a cure for arthritis."

Lumbee Ghost

aybe you saw a news story a while back about a hostage-taking by a pair of Indians down our way. It seems that, even here in 1988, the Lumbee Indians of North Carolina's Robeson County felt put upon by a white political structure, and two supporters took over the local newspaper office. It caused quite a stir and made the national press, which was all the young braves wanted anyway. They got arrested, and no one got hurt.

But the story dragged me back in time to the era between World War II and the Korean war when I bird hunted a lot down that way. A then young, white lawyer from the city took gun and dogs into that county only by sufferance. Which meant you'd be going by invitation with local friends or you were likely to find your tires—or even your precious hide—cut up a bit. It's always been a violent county, and the area around the little town of Pembroke was not posted with welcome signs.

I was lucky and privileged to know some of those folks, and was always treated warmly and courteously. I wasn't free-lance writing at the time, or I would have told this tale long ago. Even now, you the reader are going to help me sort it out. I'm not sure myself, whether this is fact or fiction.

After the Big War, I'd made the acquaintance of Billy Oxendine (another G. I., but he much decorated) at veterans' and political gatherings where we laid grandiose plans to take over state politics from the Old Guard. Pending a decision as to which of us ought to be the next governor, we did some serious bird hunting in his territory, because that's where the quail were. The area is flat, black land interspersed with creeks, swamps, and row crops, drained by the Lumbee River. Flat? Flat enough so the railroad that ran through Moss Neck covered more than seventy miles without a single curve. Swampy? I can count Long Swamp, Bear, Black, and Saddletree, just to name a few.

If you're going to insert yourself deeply into this story, bear with me for a little historical perspective. It was this miasmic country of canebrakes and moss-draped bald cypresses to which fled, strangely enough, remnants of a tribe of Sioux Indians, far from their plainsmen kin, when caught between the powerful Tuscarora and warlike Cherokee at about the time the first whites settled on the Carolina coast. There is even a legend that John White's lost colony may have melded into what has now been legislatively named the Lumbee tribe, accounting for gray-eyed Indians reported by John Lawson in the early eighteenth century.

And Robeson was the hideaway for the Lowrie gang that terrorized the countryside from 1865 to about 1875. Henry Berry Lowrie was its leader and is still the patron saint and legendary Robin Hood of the Lumbees; these swamps were his Sherwood Forest. Historians tell us his father and brother were tied to a stake and executed without trial by the local home guard in the last year of the War Between the States. His mother and sister watched from a corn crib, identifying thirteen whites. And his mother, when Henry learned of the lynching and vowed vengeance, asked her son to spare only one of the participants, a man who had tried to stop the killing. The press of that decade is full of accounts of how Henry Berry and a handful of friends, in revenge, spent ten years in ambush and counterattack, until, by attrition, the combatants on both sides (including twelve of the original home guardsmen) were wiped out. Henry Berry disappeared mysteriously from the county, a vanishing act still unexplained by the history books.

But Billy and I were not thinking about history when we left his house in Pembroke that December afternoon. I had brought down a dead-white setter bitch named Sue and a mean, hard-headed pointer named Frank. We left Billy's dogs at the house because Frank would fight anything up to and including a boar-hog. The dogs made a good team, Frank being the wide-ranging covey dog and Sue deadly on singles and a good retriever. It had been cold that morning, but as sometimes happens in the Carolinas, positively shirt-sleeve weather by midday.

We worked the edges of some beanfields, nailing a couple of coveys in the first hour and picking up four or five birds. Which was pretty good for that early in the day and bode well for later in the afternoon. The third bevy flushed wild ahead of the dogs and flew into what we called flat-piney woods, across culti-vated fields, a quarter-mile away. I had learned early on that Robeson quail don't sit down close by. So we went back to the truck, drank a pop, smoked a ciga-rette, and leisurely made our way by farm road to near where the pines flanked a little swamp. The trees were eighty-foot loblolly, and somehow looked dark and forbidding, probably, I thought later, be-cause a cold front was laying down black clouds which distorted the light quality.

But it had been a big covey and we had marked its entry by a dead snag, so we were pretty sure of some good singles shooting before weather struck, and be-fore getting into the swamp thickets. Parking and off-loading the dogs, we cast them on, jumped the roadside ditch, and loaded up.

We were not more than a hundred yards into the woods when we came upon a strangely dressed old In-dian, chopping out lightard stumps. For you non-natives, "lightard" is colloquial for "lightwood," old heart pine from trees tapped in the last century for turpentine. It's full of pitch, makes great kindling, and poor folks used it for indoor lighting when they couldn't afford kerosene for the lamps. My dad, who ultimately turned out to be a federal judge, told me many times that he studied his lessons at night by the light of a lightard knot. So it was not unusual for a local to be gathering an armful here in early winter. It was the clothing that somehow looked out of place. You've seen it in illustrations from old hunting magazines: musty long-lapelled jacket, shirt collar buttoned but no tie, dark wool britches string-wrapped below the knee like leggings, and shapeless felt hat. His face was dark copper, deeply lined and wrinkled. Hair, still coal-black, poked from beneath the hatbrim but failed to cover a dark-red welt on the neck beneath the jaw.

Billy, still the politician, stopped and spoke. "Howdy," he said. "I'm Billy Oxendine from over to Pembroke and this is Dave Henderson from Charlotte. I know most of the folks around here, but I don't think we've met."

The ancient one looked up from his work.

"No, but your granddaddy would have knowed me. Y'all oughten't to hunt across that swamp branch. That's sacred ground over yonder for us Lumbees. It's where Allen Lowrie raised his young uns, and them home guard killed him and his boy William. I oughta know. I rode with the Lowrie gang."

And without another word, he turned and swung his axe into a stump. He never told his name.

Well, we were too polite to laugh, so we whistled up the dogs and went on. After all, the days of the Lowrie troubles had been eight decades before, and any survivor would have had to be well over the century mark.

So we passed it off as the babbling of senility and went on with the hunt. We found some singles, crossed the branch on a fallen log, and came out into a clearing on the far side. There, under four or five old elms, was a one-story, very old, deserted cabin with a shed-roofed porch. In the yard were several out-buildings, a smoke-house, and a log corn-crib.

What we hadn't noticed in the cover of the timber was the advent of the promised storm. An early December thunderstorm, while rare, can be deadly in these climes. Suddenly a blast of wind struck, followed by an instant downpour. We started to run for the shelter of the porch when there in front of us, half-hidden by the streaking rain and mist, appeared a dozen or so figures, most with guns, and two others obviously tied up to a post. Just as the mob raised the guns to a shooting position, a terrible clap of thunder split the sky, lightning struck one of the trees, and—Well. . . .

I don't yet know which of us first found the log across the creek. Frank, the bold pointer, had his hackles up and his tail between his legs when he passed me. Sue was a white streak somewhere up front. Billy and I were side by side making like a pair of Olympic hurdlers when we came out of the swamp back into the pines. I remember noticing that the old man was nowhere to be seen, but his old hand-forged axe was stuck into a stump. Then we were at the truck, breathless and with, I'm sure, sheepish looks on our faces.

The next week, in the mail from Billy, was a clipping from his local paper: "A lightning-set fire from an unpredicted winter thunderstorm destroyed a patch of timber on the run of Bear Swamp. The fire burned up to the foundation of the historic Allen Lowrie cabin but was miraculously extinguished without damaging the structure."

Now, I'm pretty skeptical about the occult, ESP, precognition, witchcraft, and contacts with the afterlife, and not quite sure of what we had heard and seen or *thought* we had heard and seen. But I was intrigued by the references to the Lowrie gang, so I went to the source to read more about it in a Lumbee history, *The Only Land I Know,* by Dr. Adolph Dial, a professor at Pembroke University. What I found was even more frightening. Because on page 73 of the book, this appeared:

On March 17, 1871, at precisely 12:30 p.m., the trap fell, and Henderson Oxendine became the only member of the Lowrie gang to be executed publicly. There was no attempt at rescue.

Shades of Rod Serling and the Twilight Zone! Two bird-hunting guys, Dave *Henderson* and Billy *Oxendine* meet an old Indian with a red welt on his neck, claiming to have been a member of the gang, though the history book says the last member was hanged, and his name was *Henderson Oxendine.* Coincidence? Or had we seen the Lumbee Ghost?

Walker's Pointer

o a passer-by, the stranger would appear to be fifty, maybe fifty-two. But there was no mistaking his athlete's shoulders, hard waist, and tight buttocks. Mostly it was his eyes that betrayed his years—the eyes and the tired lines around his mouth that spoke of emotional hard times. A Jones-style camo hat covered most of the frosting on the black hair. He sat alone in the back booth at the Lake Tahoma Lodge dining room. He had eaten there almost every night that November. Obviously not a mountain man, he'd seen little sign of hospitality except a few kind words from Eva, the waitress.

Up front, the regulars gathered nightly. Old Man Miller, his sons and son-in-law, neighbors from the surrounding hills, they were bearhunters to a man. One of them, a fellow called Buck Doone from up around Spruce Pine, told the funniest stories the stranger had ever heard, and the whole crowd guffawed and slapped thighs—having a high old time.

The bear-hunting season was upon them. Here in the Smokies, on the "front side" of Mt. Mitchell, highest peak east of the Rockies, the Lodge was the court and Mr. Miller was the King. He was hard as a hickory knot at seventy years of age, and he had worn the crown for half a century. The wall of the Lodge was graced by two huge black-bear hides, one of them squaring almost eight feet.

There were tales of a spring bear hunt in Michigan when the crowd had killed nine bear, and recollections of times when Judge Bill Anglin closed court on Friday at noon, helped them load the dogs, and headed with them for the coastal swamps to hunt two days straight with no sleep, returning just in time to open court on Monday morning. Oh, there were stories of Plotts, blueticks, redbones, and the fighting Airedales, and confrontations with the revenooers who had plagued the hillfolks years ago. They had the comradeship of long association, old family ties, and the Southern mountaineers' inherent suspicion of strangers. In all, they were a rough, macho lot, a fraternity of harddrinking (red stuff, now) and hard-hunting buddies.

More than anything, Ed Walker, the man in the back booth, longed to join them. The truth is the man was lonely—lonely from what he had been through, and lonely shut out as he was from a group of hunters. He wasn't used to it, or hadn't been until lately.

If someone from the crowd had checked on him, which they certainly would have done back when the

Revenue boys were working the hollows, things might have been different. Ed was from a little town near the coast. After his parents were killed in a wreck, he had been reared by his Uncle Bob. From the time the boy could shoulder a shotgun, the uncle had taught him more about the outdoors than probably any kid had learned since Ruark's Old Man was tutor to The Boy.

They had hunted and fished for every type of game, including bear, had learned sign, gotten wet, frozen their toes; and the boy became a complete outdoorsman. Of course, they always came back to quail, Uncle Bob's first love, mostly because of the dogs. It was the birddogs that were Ed's passion. But then he got a football scholarship at, of all places, the mountain school, Appalachian State. It was here right under the noses of this Tahoma crowd. There he'd made Little All-American. That, he thought, might have earned him at least a "hello."

After college, it was back East, marrying Ellen from down the block, watching two kids get grown, and doing reasonably well selling insurance. That was a job that let him capitalize on old friends, and at the same time hunt and fish. He was out every weekend and a couple of afternoons a week. It should, perhaps, have come as no surprise when, after twenty-five years of being full-time mother and part-time father, Ellen woke him at two o'clock one morning to announce that she was resigning both jobs. "Tired of being a hunting widow," she said, and besides, the new vice-president at the bank is "kind, thoughtful, likes to travel, and very much in love with me."

So, with half the proceeds of the sale of the house, his insurance residuals, his shotgun, and the older Pontiac, he thought he could make it until Social Security. He added to the cash by selling his two setters, both solid-broke, for fifteen hundred apiece. Before the tears could start, he loaded the pointer, up front beside him as usual, and headed back to the hills, the hills where he had had his greatest successes. With a dog that loved him, if nobody else did.

About the dog, which I've been a long time getting around to. Bo was five, white with liver ears, White Knight breeding, but with blockier head. The chest was deep and full, and even now at the end of the summer the muscular structure still stood out like that of an iron-pumping beach-boy. He was one of those all-day-on-the-ground dogs, disdaining the breaks afforded the setters. His stamina was superb, and he was the best birddog Ed had ever seen. Even in new territory where the ground stayed in continuous tilt, where quail were scarce, and where grouse were king, Ed thought the dog would do all right.

He bought a lot just off the highway, fenced the back half (which was futile, because Bo thought a six-foot barrier was fun to climb), and put in a one-bedroom house-trailer. There'd be time after hunting season to find work—if he had to. Bo ended up sleeping inside and they were together constantly. In the daytime, they scouted territory, adjusting muscles from flat-country beanfields to rugged ridges, hollows that dropped a hundred feet, even rock-faces. They found grouse, but Bo didn't expect the explosions from the spruce trees, and it took him a while to shorten his range.

By opening day, he had gotten it into his head that this was a different game, and adjusted pretty well. At night, he waited in the car while Ed ate; then back to the trailer where Ed read, watched sports on the little television, moped, and brooded over the way his life had turned out.

That, then, was the situation on the first Friday in December. There'd been a dusting of snow in the Catawba valley, and four or five inches lay at the upper levels where once ranged cougar, wolves, and wapiti. Now the game was European boar, lesser feral hogs, black bear, and ruffed grouse. On a step forty or fifty yards wide, Ed and Bo were working the edge of a stand of rare Frazier fir, staying on the high side of a laurel hell that spilled down the slope. They were halfway up toward the Eastern Continental Divide, maybe at three thousand feet. Ed carried the Browning Citori 12, wearing the short set of barrels in this thick, strange country where twenty yards was about maximum range. The gun was his last extravagance, perhaps the straw that sent Ellen away. By ten o'clock a mist was lifting and two birds were in the game bag. One to go on the limit, and Ed had regained a little of his zest for living.

A rock outcrop blocked their progress, and when Ed clambered to the top he was surprised to hear hound-music, obviously in hot pursuit and just as surely working up a shoulder in his direction. Still, he guessed, a half-hour off. He was about to sit down to see the show when, not fifty yards below him, out of the cover of a long-dead chestnut tree, stepped another hunter. Rifle at ready, anticipating a bear, there, unmistakably, was Old Man Miller. Hurrying, he missed his footing on an ice-covered rock, went down on his knees, and lost hold on his weapon.

And there, barreling through the laurel, huffing like a logging engine, came the bear. It was just a medium-sized boar-bear, no magazine-cover grizzly, but it was one angry Eastern black, enraged at having been rousted from its lay-out den. Swinging only slightly off course, it grabbed the man by the shoulder.

Bo, already halfway down the slope, chose to inter-vene. Genetics, that wonderfully reliable discipline, de-termines inherited traits, and it is to be remembered that the English pointer, according to the literature, carries in his veins the genes of the pit-bull. Bear-baiting, with that breed, goes back hundreds of years. So perhaps Ed should have anticipated what was about to happen as he shucked out his number sixes and, on a dead run, thumbed in a pair of double-ought bucks he kept in his pocket against an attack by hogs. But Bo arrived before him, launching straight for the bear's jaw, just below the ear—the classic "catch-hold," safe from the bear's teeth and inside the radius of the deadly front claws, the instinctive assault tactic of his bear-baiting ancestors. Despite the bear's thick fur, it must have hurt. Some say the pit-bull's jaws exert a pressure of 1800 pounds per square inch. Be that as it may, the bear dropped his victim and spun, trying to rid himself of this seventy-pound attacker. Ed couldn't shoot for fear of hitting his dog. He didn't see the old man rising again to his knees, unsheathing a Bowie knife with his left hand. As bear and dog rolled toward him, the mountain man picked his spot and buried the long blade in the black belly. The battle was over.

The old man's rawhide, fleece-lined coat, its right sleeve now torn out, had almost saved the flesh, but blood seeped through the shirt. Miller, again with his left hand, reached into the pocket of his denim over-alls, extracted a pint bottle of clear liquid, and poured it over his shoulder, shirt and all. For the first time, then, he seemed to notice Ed, who was checking to see that Bo was all right.

"Hey, ain't you the flatlander I've seed over at the Lodge? I'd be glad if you'd join me in a drink of these corn-squeezin's. I'd offer one to your dog if I thought he'd take it. And if them other dogs and fellers ever get here, maybe you'd like to join up with us. There's an-other bear on the back side of the mountain."

Dog's Life

ome human, thinking himself pretty much a smart-ass in the outdoor writing field, is always trying to write as though he is himself a dog. Can't be done. They don't know dogtalk.

My name is Dan when I'm working, but formally it's Dave's Dashing Dan, and I carry a pretty good pedigree as a Llewellin setter, a breed listed with The American Field. That's a better bloodline and more than I can say for a lot of the guys that come to Briarpatch Farms to bird hunt. I was kidnapped when I was only about eight weeks old and brought here by a man named Dave, but that I call "Bossman" because he's been bossing me around ever since. Not that such has been a tough life, as you'll see.

I vaguely remember his coming a couple times to the kennel where I was whelped (now there's a dog word), looking at my brothers and sisters and me, and finally saying to some big, rough looking fellow, "I'll take that one as pick of the litter," and then scooping me up in a huge man's hand. He rubbed me up behind the ears (I've always been a sucker for that) and off we went, leaving Mama and the kids behind. If I ever saw any of them again, I don't know it. I had already begun to drink from a pan, and was what men called "about weaned," meaning I could get along without Mama's milk, and eat puppy chow.

The kennels at Briarpatch were gravel bottomed when first I moved in, but Bossman later concreted the runs, and it was easier on a dog's feet, if a little slick after a rain. In the run next to mine were two pointer youngsters, about three months old, I'd guess. I was to get to know them well in the next five or six years, because we trained together, and later hunted together all over the area. But they don't talk much, and lack good conversational skills, anyway.

One of the myths men pass along is that pointers learn bird hunting quicker than setters. Bull bullets! I never let those pups named Tip and Tuck, get ahead of me on anything. Oh, maybe right at first, because they were older, but later, I could match anything they did and do it a little better. You don't mind a little family pride, do you?

Bossman had fixed up a box with a little ramp in front of the door so I could get in and out. It was Spring, and he didn't keep much straw inside, but it was fun to drag out whatever he stuck in. My coat was just beginning to thicken, and by Fall, Bosslady said I was the prettiest dog she'd ever seen. That was one day when the sun was behind me and she stuck a black box out toward me and clicked it. She was always talking about "backlighting," and my picture appeared on the front of one of the national niche magazines, but that was all in the future.

I'd been "in residence" only a couple weeks when

Bossman lifted me over the gate and put me down in the huge backyard. Boy, it was great to run, but I felt pretty comfortable when I got back to him, because there was that scratching behind the ears again, and a goodie to boot. Then the most marvelous thing happened. He hung this delicious smell on the end of a string tied to a pole of some sort. I took one sniff, and something came back, probably from my great, great grandfather, and my back stiffened, my little ole tail went stiff, and I raised my right foot. I don't know why it happened, but it just seemed natural. Bossman moved the brown feathers, but I felt frozen. He moved it again, and I thought it was going to get away but he made it hard to catch. Then he stopped it again, right in front of my nose, and I couldn't move a muscle. Bossman seemed mightily pleased.

All that summer we worked with the feathers, and what he called "yard training." Some of it seemed a bit silly, like having to walk only on his left side when he said "heel," but a couple of pops across my nose with the lead line, and I got the idea in a hurry. I heard him say to the yardman that I didn't need something he called "forced retrieving," but I already thought it was fun to fetch anything he threw, and especially a frozen bunch of feathers he called a "bird." I'm glad he couldn't understand dog-talk, because some of the things I called him when we were doing his "sit-stay" business would have gotten my butt whipped. But I finally satisfied the guy on "come," and "sit-stay," "loadup," and "whoa!" even when there were no feathers out front.

I haven't told you about Ranger and Sis. They were big dogs that lived with us, but got to ride in the truck a lot when the weather began to get brisk. I really liked that truck. Loading up meant we were about to go somewhere where a dog could run. Sometimes I went with them, but first I had to learn what that blamed whistle meant. Seemed like it always came with "whoa!" but I was off there where He couldn't reach me, and chasing stinkbirds was a lot of fun. There came the day when I paid no attention and the new collar around my neck suddenly bit like a bumble bee, so I hustled back to the Man. He ruffed me up a little, and mumbled something about modern technology.

One day when I was running loose, I smelled that grand odor of feathers, but it didn't want to play, and a dozen bombshells blasted it out from under my nose. There went that whistle and bumble bee again and Bossman hollering "whoa!" and my chase was over. Later, I was working behind Sis one day and she stopped dead still, but there was that bird smell in front of her, and I stopped to see what was up. It was those bombshells again, but not until the Man had walked past me and then Sis, and his black stick made a whale of a bang. Sis went out and brought back two birds.

The noise didn't bother me. I'd had a lot of pan-banging at feeding time, and we'd hear that Man's short black stick pop pretty loudly when I was out with the pointer pups. What it did was mighty exciting, because next time it happened, I was the dog out front, my nose was full of those grand smells, and Ranger stopped behind me, and here came Bossman with the long stick, and bang!, bang! Then I found what he was after, and brought him a dead feathers that was not frozen at all, but still hot. He must have been really proud of me, because he rubbed me up, and whispered in my ear, and I rode home in the cab of the truck.

There were times when we went to a vet, and got a lot of needles and a probe up my hindend, but all the dogs went, so it wasn't punishment. I learned some human words there. One of them was "pheromones," which meant an even grander smell than quail birds. A couple of teachers-types were talking, and said that female humans once put out those invitations, but that some dame in Egypt named Cleopatra, who had a loveboat, tried to cover up with frankincense and myrrh, whatever those were. Not that she succeeded, but she set a bad pattern.

I'm glad lady dogs don't carry on such foolishness. You see, once when I was about three, a visiting truck pulled up at the kennel, and the most delicious pheromones ever came wafting my way. It turns out I was elected, undoubtedly because of my handsomeness, to play host to a lady from another kennel. Left in the run with me, she was somewhat standoffish, and at first nearly snapped my head off. But I sweet-talked her, nuzzled her all over, and suddenly we were in love. Boy!, I don't know why they kept this a secret. Sometimes a dog's life ain't too bad!

Our principal business, though, was finding, pointing, and holding quail, and then retrieving. I once stopped in the afternoon to try to see how good one would taste. Just once! The man was on me like a cloud of yellow jackets, and I said, "Well, if you're that selfish, you can have 'em all."

I didn't go with the pointers to the field trials. I'm a proud foot-hunting dog with Gladstone and Count Noble in my line. I learned my job and do it darn well.

But that's how it's been and each to his own. I guess I really love old Boss, in spite of that collar, now that I'm the dog that always rides in the cab.

Rebel's Rest

he sharp little Mazda RX7 was cruising at just short of seventy-five when Bob saw the sign. He was half a mile past before it registered and he brought the slick sports car to a stop on the shoulder. The arrow had pointed from a farm road with an open aluminum gate, and the notice had said "Field Trial."

On a late February morning, Bob Johnson was heading for the capital. The case he was to argue was first on Friday's docket, but the pressures of the office had everybody on the screaming edge, so he had signed himself out and left for the capital a day early to loosen up a bit and hone his oral argument. He had planned to check in early at the Hilton, which was within walking distance of the court where he had to be the next morning. He'd have a drink, a steak at the client's expense, then take a couple of hours to review his brief, and maybe, just maybe, get a good night's sleep. That would be pretty rare at a time when things were breaking so fast at the firm. There had been three mergers in the five years since he and Peggy had broken up—divorced. Now there were half a hundred lawyers in the organization, and the end was not in sight. But this was what he wanted, the challenge, the success, the power, and, of course, the big money. He was now a partner, with a chance this year of having his name added on the door. And he had been named managing partner of the new Charlotte office, already bursting its quarters and carrying six other lawyers and a dozen support personnel. He was thinking of trading the Mazda for that Porsche he'd tested last week. And he was only thirty-eight years old.

"What the hell," he said to himself. "Take a break." It had been years since he'd been to a trial. Now he scarcely had time for three or four hunts a season, and his old dog Rebel, who had once earned a lot of trophies, was badly stove up with arthritis and obviously wouldn't be around for another winter. "Sad," he mused, "no more bird hunting and pretty damned lonely next fall. There'll be no yip from the kennel when I get home at ten or eleven, no wagging tail, and nobody home to really give a cuss." So he did a one-eighty and turned in at the gate.

Near the registration tent he pulled the car in under some maples, reached into the back and pulled from his duffel bag a pair of Wellingtons to replace the high-shine mahogany loafers. He unknotted his tie, shed his jacket, and pulled on a light blue mohair sweater. Then he just sat for a while, memories flooding over him. Peggy had given him that sweater on their last Christmas. There had been three years of heaven and hell, about equally balanced, he thought. Before, he had been practicing law three or four years, making a pretty hot name for himself in trial work, and had just won his first hundred-thousand-dollar verdict. The fee, on a contingency of a third, had seemed enormous to him. He was off to the races!

The following weekend, at a college football game, somebody introduced him at the fraternity house to a bubbling, fresh-faced, gorgeously engineered girl. She was still wearing a monogrammed sweatshirt which utterly failed to disguise her femininity, and the shorts—well! She'd been out in a pickup field-hockey game just for the zest of it, even though she was a graduate student working on her doctorate in animal husbandry.

The honeymoon had been marvelous, and the marriage, for a while, made in heaven. They both had liked the outdoors, hunting and fishing. Coming from a rural background and a hunting heritage, she adored Rebel and the field trials Bob introduced her to. She was there when they picked up their first puppy-stakes trophy and she was there again and again until the mantel was covered with shooting-dog awards won by the precocious Rebel.

But the ambitious young attorney discovered that the law was a jealous mistress that left less and less time for the dog and for Peggy. Then came the offer to join a ten-man group in a larger city. Peggy was loyal, but moved only reluctantly. Next, an even bigger, high-tech firm took over, and there seemed to be no free time at all. He wanted a condo and a Mercedes; she wanted a house in the middle of fifty acres and a pickup truck. They parted and, with no children, the divorce was mechanical. Peggy was independent and undemanding, quickly finding work in a new laboratory near her parents' home in the center of the state. There had been no communication, not even a Christmas card. Bob, except for a few one-night stands, spent practically all his time at the office.

So it was with a sense of *deja vu* that he pulled on an old Red Man cap and wandered over to where the crowd was watching a brace working the birdfield. It was one of those local trial clubs, probably not sanctioned, with a course run for half an hour, handlers on foot, judges on horseback, ending at the birdfield with a designated shooter. There was a point, a good back, the crack of the shotgun, and a nice retrieve. A shiver went over the young man and he felt his heart make an extra beat.

Some entrepreneur had trailered in half a dozen horses for rent to spectators who wanted to follow the dogs. On impulse, Bob handed over two dollars and threw a leg over a slightly swaybacked roan gelding. Its gait was surprisingly good, a smooth mid-paced trail walk, as Bob moved over to the group gathered behind the judges.

A new brace was being put down, derbies, the last before lunch—two gyps, a pointer and a setter, both alert and pressing against the leads. It was the setter, though, that caught his eye. Almost solid white with dark tan ears. Bob immediately thought, "Thor breeding," and wondered that he even remembered bloodlines or could identify characteristics. There had been times when he and Peggy had shared these outings, talking to hunters, breeders, and other dog-folks, learning a lot together, laughing with the wins and sometimes almost crying in disappointment. Lovely days. Gone days.

He glanced at the program. She was listed only as "Judy," owned and handled by John Locklear. "Lumbee Indian," John thought. "Always good with bird dogs." They were off, and for the first time in months Bob felt a lift of spirit. The dogs moved out, followed by the judges and observers, and it was a good race, both dogs working well, with little to choose between them. In the birdfield, though, the setter took charge, had three finds, backed perfectly when required, and retrieved to hand. It was almost like the first time he had seen Peggy; here was something he simply had to have.

There was no logic in acquiring another dog, but logic was irrelevant. At the barbecue lunch he sidled up to Locklear. "Know anybody around who might want to unload a young dog before summer?" he said.

"Never wanted to get rid of one I raised," Locklear said, "but I breed 'em, break 'em, and sell 'em. You want that Judy dog." It was a conclusion, not a question, and the negotiations were brief. The breeder got a hundred and a half more than he would have sold for the day before, Bob paid a hundred and a half less than he would have been willing to spend to get the dog.

Bob said, "Two weeks' trial. If the dog's got heart-worms, it's your dog and my money back. If the dog gets killed, stolen, or runs off, it's my dog and your money. Fair enough?"

"Standard with me," said Locklear, and wrote down his address and phone number.

"Mail me back the collar. You keep the lead."

Judy loaded on command, curled up in the jumpseat, and quietly licked the big hand that gently roughed her ears. She must have been surprised on the road to Raleigh that the driver was singing at the top of his voice. Lodged overnight in the kennel of a local vet, she was ready for the drive home after court next day. There Bob introduced her to old Rebel, who seemed pleased enough. On Saturday he enlarged the pen in the tiny backyard.

There was one more Saturday to hunt, and the two new companions took full advantage of it. A bond seemed to have been quickly established between them and the day went well, Judy almost perfection as a walk-and-hunt dog. That summer, golf with rich clients markedly diminished. Bob often left the office early. The pair wandered woodlands, swam creeks, fought briers just for the hell of it. The man's face and arms tanned, his legs came back, and he felt alive. Judy thrived on his affection. When the field-trial season opened in October, Bob felt guilty at not letting his girl-dog reach her potential so he made inquiries, joined a little N.B.H.A club, and devoted time to sharpening her skills. There wasn't time for hunting, but with new friends, the renewal of his hobby, and Judy's successes, the fall passed quickly.

Somehow, the office didn't seem so important. The setter won firsts at two of the derby events, placed every time she was entered, and was beginning to cause comments as the dog to beat whenever she showed up. She was running out of derby age, so Bob entered her in the home club December shooting-dog trial against some very good competition. When she took first place, he was ecstatic.

There were motions to be heard in superior court at Southern Pines, a hundred miles east, on a Friday morning in January. Coincidentally, N.B.H.A. was scheduling a regional trial that same weekend at nearby Hoffman. Why not, thought Bob, take a flier with Judy at bigger game? He could easily have sent one of his junior lawyers to make the court appearances, but decided to go himself, take Judy, and enter her as a shooting dog. It would be good experience for a young dog and a break for him here in winter. He mailed in the entry fee, sent Judy down ahead with a buddy who was alerted that Bob might be delayed and miss the drawing. Then he met his commitment to his client.

The hearings dragged on, and the drawing was held before he got out of court. Unable to locate his friend that night, he was unprepared for what he saw next morning at the clubhouse. There on the bulletin board, along with pictures of the great champions from the big field trials of years past, was the program for the two-day regional. Puppies and derbies had been run on Friday, and the shooting-dog stakes would begin at ten o'clock, delayed by a heavy morning fog. His eye ran down the pairings—damn! He and Judy were scheduled to run against—he could not believe what he was reading. "Third brace: Judy owned and handled by Bob Johnson; Rebel owned and handled by Peggy Johnson."

Not his Peggy! Not his used-to-be Peggy! She didn't live very far away, but he didn't know she even owned a dog. Except, of course, that blasted dachshund she used to have that threatened to bite him every time he'd patted her pretty behind—the one he'd called "Attila." And she'd even stolen old Rebel's name for her entry. By God, he'd just forfeit. Damned if he'd compete with *her!* But then he thought, damned if he'd let her get away with it! Of course, there needn't be any confrontation, he had no wish for an ugly scene. He brought Judy to the line at the last moment, and the two handlers avoided eye-contact, each with set jaw and apparent exclusive interest in their charges. Peggy's dog was a handsome male setter, lightly ticked.

Old Judge Beachum (who really had once been a judge) and Will Lippard, a knowledgeable dog man, were the judges, both well mounted and experienced. Beachum had known Bob and Peggy from the years they were a team, and he seemed a bit bemused.

At "Loose your dogs," both entrants were off and running. Rebel took the top side of a beanfield along the edge of a pine woods. Judy elected to work left, down a broad hedgerow, settling into her slow canter that Bob, as a birdhunter, thought so beautiful. Rebel was covering ground. He had rounded the field and was coming downwind on the hedgerow when Judy pointed. Rebel sight-backed, pretty as you please. Judy had a single from birds put out for a prior brace. Bob marked, shot, and Judy retrieved. Steady to wing and shot was not required. Rebel held until Peggy called him off—both dogs perfect, but Judy credited with the find. The whole half hour was crowded with good dog work. It was unlikely that anything else entered that day could surpass this performance. Two wild coveys graced the course. Each dog had a find, and each time the other backed. Only a slight indiscretion marked the run. A single bird ran on Judy, and she might, just might, have moved to relocate before Bob's command.

The dogs were picked up and the antagonists left the field separately to await the decisions later in the day. With the trial completed, the trialmaster's bullhorn called to the trophy table one Sam Davis, Peggy Johnson, and Bob Johnson. Davis, in inverse order, got third place with his pointer, Sam, Jr. The tension was obvious to the onlookers, who by this time had passed among themselves the whole little melodrama. Judge Beachum, studiously looking over the heads of the handlers, intoned, "The judges have had a difficult time differentiating between these two fine performances. Except for one slight miscalculation"—he paused—"these dogs were dead even. We must, however, award second place to Johnson's Judy and first place to Johnson's Rebel."

The man and the woman, for the first time, looked at each other. "Well," said Bob, "it's time a male won." He grinned at her as he spoke, and added, "C'm on, I'll buy you a beer." As they walked off together, old Beachum grinned, too, and quoted that venerable observation, attributed to the Governors of North and South Carolina, "It's a long time between drinks—a damned long time."

Postscript: In the June 19th issue of the Southern Pines *Pilot* there appeared a small news item. "The community welcomes, as newcomers, Mr. and Mrs. Robert Johnson. Mr. Johnson has announced that he is opening an office in the Smith Building for the practice of law. He comes here from a large firm in Charlotte. Mrs. Johnson will operate a breeding and training kennel for pointers and setters at their country home, Rebel's Rest."

Santee Sleuth

arry Gasque and his Lab, Brant, found the body on a Monday morning, just at daylight. It was truly happenstance, because it was unlikely that Larry or anybody else would be fishing that day in the stickups off the "subdivision," that area known to all Santee-Cooper bass fishermen that lies on the west side of the lower lake, south of the diversion canal. The wind was wrong, and only a very knowledgeable "local" would have been able to find his way through the stump field to the protected waters where there were still evidences of the willows that had been inundated years before.

It was still, on a June day in 1985, a likely place for a lunker to strike a top-water lure in early morning. Larry was rigged with a silver Diamondback Rattler, the same lure Odell Haire had used years before in the same neighborhood, in taking a nine-pounder. Odell had struck so hard, he'd ripped the ferrules off a good Fenwick rod. Larry remembered, because he had just moved up from

Florida, and there was a lot of talk at the lake marinas about Haire's prowess.

Now about forty, Larry had been born in Georgetown, only twenty-five miles from the lakes, and had spent his boyhood fishing Winyah Bay and the Waccamaw, Black, and PeeDee rivers, with occasional forays to the big lakes. Love of the outdoors interfered with a lot of formal education, but everybody knew him for a smart kid, with a lot of savvy about hunting and fishing, and about the most observant guy around. He seemed to see and know every moving thing, from hoppy-toads to bald eagles. His curiosity was legend; if he couldn't explain what was happening out there, he'd spend hours reading on the subject at the Georgetown library. A bit of a loner, but that's not to say he didn't have friends. As a matter of fact, he'd spent one summer being a beach bum at Myrtle, waiting tables in the daytime and shagging with the teenage crowd all night at the Pavilion. That's where he'd met Sarah, followed her back to Florida, and there got married.

For a couple of years he had been a bass guide on the St. John and in and around the Basin. Tragedy struck when Sarah, newly pregnant, one day slipped and fell at the boat dock. Larry lost the only things that had ever meant more to him than just being free, outdoors. His father had died, leaving him the little farm on the Waccamaw, and with the sale proceeds he'd bought a couple of acres near the settlement called Cross on the west bank of Lake Moultrie, the lower impoundment of the Santee-Cooper power project. There he built a neat cottage, set up a garden and dogpens, and bought himself a nineteen-foot open guide boat, later traded for a utility-grade bass boat when those specialized, swivel-seated, low-gunnel fish-killers came on the market. His was not a glitter-job, but camo, because he guided for ducks as well as fish.

Of late, he had been working stripers, and even the huge blue catfish, because the big gatemouths had, in his opinion, been pretty well wiped out by the constant bass-tournament pressure. He didn't like the concept, although he forgave his young friend Terry Roberts because he needed the money and the prizes were enormous. There had been such a "contest" over the weekend. Terry had participated, but Larry hadn't heard the results.

That Monday morning, Brant spotted the undulations of the wavelets around a strange, log-like object. At first, Larry thought it must be a gator lying in the shallows. It would have had to be a big one, more than six feet, but that wouldn't be especially rare, although this was pretty near the northernmost range for the really big ones. Brant was the big Lab that, as a puppy, was one of a series of retrievers at Larry's, always acquired in an effort to stave off loneliness. Now, at seventy-five pounds, only this successor was the man's constant companion, known by every native on both lakes as the best water dog around. A faultless retriever on whistle and hand-signal, he rode the front of "his" boat like a Viking figurehead, always alert for the birds, those congregations of gulls that marked fish schooling on the surface. Birds enabled striper guides to earn a living.

Larry powered the big 150 into full-up position, and as he poled inshore, thinking to sneak up on the alligator, he saw the plaid shirt, red galluses, and, of course, the beard. Piling overboard, he quickly waded to the figure. Identification was no problem; it was most certainly Bo Cadieu, a regular tournament contestant from Louisiana. When Larry turned the body over, bloody water seeped from a puncture as large as a man's finger, on top of the shoulder just where the carotid artery reaches the base of the neck. Cadieu was very, very dead.

"Well," Larry said to himself, "I guess I'm not surprised he got himself killed, but how in hell did he get out here?" He recalled first seeing the man at the tournament out of Brice's Landing the prior year. It was one of the big ones, with prizes in six figures and entrants from all over the country. Bo was there, big, bearded, obese, and obscene.

He had a girl with him, or a woman, really—Carrie something or other. Far too much quality, Larry had thought, to be following the trail with such a pig. One day she turned up with an eye pretty well purpled, but she blamed it on a door in the dark. "Door, the devil," everybody said. She was a quiet one, sitting off to the side during the weigh-in each day, always with her miniature poodle leashed or on her lap. Larry noticed her taut figure and dark-lashed eyes; he speculated that she looked as lonesome as he felt, and he empathized with her obvious love of the dog.

The final day had been memorable. Cadieu and his partner were declared the winners, coming in almost late with a gorgeous eight-pound, six-ounce sow that just beat out young Terry Roberts. Terry, whose wife was at home sick, and with three youngsters, really needed the fifteen thousand cash, and could have sold the first-place boat rig for another sixteen. He had been so close! Afterward, he groused to his older friend, saying he knew, just knew, that fat bastard had stashed that fish, tied it out somewhere and maybe even brought it in from some other state. But, of course, there was no proof.

Larry hadn't entered. He had little faith in the contention that "80 percent are live-released."

"So what? All of them turned loose at one spot in the lake, maybe three miles from the nest. No way the females don't lose their spawn."

Because he hadn't hung around this year, he didn't know that Terry and Cadieu had tangled at the dock the day before. Still nursing his year-old grudge, the younger man, against all good judgment, had accused Cadieu of cheating. Although neither was in contention for first place, the Cajun had again come in late with a big bass, and Terry just couldn't keep his mouth shut. The big man had smacked him with the back of his hand, almost knocking Terry off the dock, before the crowd separated them. The boy was livid when he got into his boat and roared off.

It was well that Larry, there in the shallow water, was strong, wiry, and in good shape. Brant was, of course, no help in hoisting two-hundred-forty-pound corpse over the low gunnels of the bass boat. Somehow he got the job done, and after marking the location with Cadieu's red suspenders tied to a buttonbush, eased out through the stumps, swung north for the diversion canal, and pulled into the mini-basin at Lyon's Landing.

An hour later, three deputy sheriffs were on hand and

waiting for the appearance of officers from SLED, the state enforcement agency. An ambulance had come across the canal bridge from the funeral home in Kingstree, and stood by, waiting for clearance from the county coroner. His preliminary report, "death from a penetration wound from an unidentified sharp object, inflicted by person or persons unknown," was just that—preliminary. But the knowledge of bad blood and the fight on the day before prompted the men from SLED to pick up Terry before noon. Protesting his innocence, he was held without bond at the little jail at Monck's Corner.

Larry was distraught. His friend, with whom he had an almost avuncular relationship, was in serious trouble, and he'd been the one who, in strange fashion, had led to the arrest. Sure, the body would have been found sooner or later, but he regretted being involved. He had escorted a small flotilla of boats full of lawmen and the curious from the landing to the place marked by the suspenders, but there was no apparent evidence of how, or why, or where Cadieu had been killed. Later, at the hatchery landing, not far from Larry's cabin, the dead man's boat was found tied up neatly at the dock. Carrie, who had been staying with him in a camping trailer nearby during the tournament, said they had come back to the trailer after the weigh-in, and he had left about nine o'clock, saying he was going to the store to have a few beers. He hadn't come home all night, she told the officers.

Larry didn't believe that Terry, hot-headed though he was, could kill anybody. It was a strange set of circumstances, anyway—no gunshot, no conventional knife wound; simply, the coroner had said, a massive puncture by a round, pointed instrument, driven deep into the shoulder. How much strength would it have taken? How could an enemy have gotten that close? How did the body get to that forsaken place?

The next day, Larry went snooping with Brant. Threading his way back to where he'd found the corpse, he sat on his front swivel seat and pondered Even if Terry had sought out Cadieu, the bigger man would never have let him get close, certainly not with any weapon shorter-ranged than a shotgun. It was only a bit later that Brant, ears up and with a slight yip, directed his attention to the birds. This time, though, they were black, not white; buzzards, not gulls. In their slow and somber airborne funeral procession, they wheeled over one of the nearby islands. Larry decided to have a look.

There, lying on the white sand beach, was a patch of black fluff. Larry tied up to a cypress sprout and waded ashore. The fluff was a miniature poodle—Carrie's much loved pup. The side of its head was bloodied, almost as if it had been crushed. The vultures had not yet gotten to its eyes. Meanwhile, Brant, who habitually spotted every movement in the water, turned his attention to a stick floating upright and causing an unnatural ripple. It was a gaff with a cork handle, floating hook down in two feet of water. "Not much doubt," thought Larry, "this was the murder weapon."

He was sure Carrie never would have let that poodle out of her possession, much less off on a jaunt with Bo alone. She must at least have been present when he died. Yet she had told the law nothing about her missing dog. As much as Larry wanted to ignore the facts, she obviously had lied about what had happened the night before. Since Cadieu would never have let anyone else aboard, there could be only one conclusion. Carrie had killed her companion.

Back at the landing, carrying the gaff with him, Larry headed straight for Cross. He had to have some explanation from this hauntingly beautiful woman who had quickly become an obsession, constantly in his thoughts. As he approached, he suddenly felt a sick, sinking sensation—the realization that he was too late. The Sheriffs deputies had already come back to Carrie's for more questioning. The boy Terry was too well known and liked to be a serious suspect, but this out-of-town woman with the sultry eyes—why that was a different matter.

Carrie was already telling her story—her confession, really—when Larry walked in. "I was down and out in Baton Rouge," she said, and her voice was unexpectedly calm, as if all her feelings were numbed. "My Dad had just died. Mom had long been gone. I was a wild one, and I couldn't take it. I went on a bad trip, a very bad trip. It was a week or so before I came out of it. I guess Bo had seen me around the wharf where Daddy worked. He bailed me out and packed me off on the circuit. He was a bum, but he fed me. He stayed in a glow all the time. We worked the tournament trail. I guess maybe it fed his ego to have me on display. That little poodle was the only touch of respectability I could hang onto. I did his laundry, cooked his meals, and took my lickings. I reckon I could take it only because he had no interest in the bedroom. He had other priorities, even though he acted super-macho. But macho or not, I never let him touch my dog.

"After the weigh-in on Sunday he was mean as a snake. That Roberts boy had caught onto Bo's bogus fish.

He'd bring them up from Georgia and tie out one or two at about every tournament. There's a livewell in back of the trailer. He had some sort of code to identify what boat-partner he drew that would cooperate in a scam. There were plenty available. They'd split the winnings, sixty-forty.

"We started out through the canal back toward the hatchery landing. Bo swung too far right, ran into a couple of stumps, and lost his bearings in the dark. And lost his temper. Somehow Feef, that's my dog, got off my lap and under his feet while he was trying to back off a submerged log. Bo went crazy. 'I always did hate this damn dog,' he said, 'and I might as well get rid of you, too. You know too much.' Then he put that big number twelve down right on my baby's head. I must have screamed. I'd picked up the gaff and when he turned on me—well, you know what happened. He fell overboard. I'd been handling that boat for three years while that bastard stole prizes. I left Feef on the island because I had nothing to bury her with. Then I flung the gaff as far as I could, picked my way out of the stumps, and ran for the landing. Shall we go now?"

The sergeant called to the jail to have Terry released. Larry watched as the car, with Carrie, drove off. Five minutes later he was at a pay phone calling Monck's Corner. "Senator, this is Larry Gasque, party chairman in your fifth precinct. Get me the best damned criminal lawyer in South Carolina."

The Valiant

he bad thing about canine fiction is the writer's proclivity to humanize his protagonist. Indeed, escaping anthropomorphism is so difficult, a story about a dog almost always turns out to be about Lassie, or Rin-tin-tin, or Ole Joe, who—or more properly, which—takes on the character of a young girl, or a Western hero, or your strange but gifted uncle. Lest you overempathize with the principal character of this piece, I've named him ("him" because he's male) simply: Dog.

Dog was a pointer of regal breeding, whelped to the purple, silver chewing bone in his jaw, to the super kennel born, and equipped with all other such evidence that this will not be a rags-to-riches story. He was trained as a shooting dog, of course, and all the inherent instinct of his tribe made him a prodigy, the pride of his boss, George, and talk of the hunt club before he was two.

George had taken him home at eight weeks, and, contrary to the belief of some, house-dog and hunting companion were truly one. The lady of the house adopted the puppy, "staying home," as she put it, for the two or three weeks it took for housebreaking. And since George traveled during the week, to her fell the daily stint of keeping the yard training an ongoing thing.

Weekends, though, belonged to George and Dog. They rode in the pickup, worked on the feather, took long walks to teach the youngster how to quarter, taught and learned "whoa!" (Come October, Dog was off to Bolich's to fine-tune the promise, and the professional did his job. By season's opener, the student had become a proficient bird dog.

Back at the ranch, or rather at George and Lady's house, somewhat unexpectedly for a middle-aged couple, came a new member to the household. Beth was red and wrinkled, made strange noises, and, to Dog, smelled bad. She also pre-empted him in terms of attention from his folks. It was not the best of times, but the hunting took out some of the sting. Dog seemed to throw himself into the sport. He worked—oh, how he worked—to please. Tail bloodied, he hit the briars. He ran the edges, found, pointed, and retrieved. With Bolich, the pro, who came along because he liked to see Dog perform, and his friend Skinny, George took every opportunity the second season to be in the quail fields. Lady and Beth were doing well, and the little one was beginning to toddle. The territory George serviced was prospering, and the extra money made it easier to take time out for hunting. Birds were relatively plentiful, and it was a very good season.

Late in December down near Pineville, the three hunting buddies, as they frequently did, hopscotched an area of beanfields, broomstraw, a patch of cut-over pine with a sawdust pile, a cemetery, and a couple of old house sites. Two hunters and three dogs would take a turn while the third would parallel with the truck and relief dogs. On this day, Skinny was on the truck and had pulled up at the rendezvous. He was sitting on the tailgate lighting his pipe when he heard George calls "Have you seen Dog?" Bolich came up, the two dogs present kenneled, and George hit the whistle. Rarely had he resorted to blowing, because Dog checked in so regularly you could almost set your watch by him.

Obviously, something was wrong. Bolich, veteran bird hunter, first voiced the real concern—old house site, open well. Skinny gunned the old truck straight through a barbed-wire fence, ran over a dozen saplings, and skidded into the yard of a deserted tenant house. There, the rock casement fallen in, was the well. Shallow but deadly—for fifteen feet down in the rubble, there was Dog. And with him was a two-foot copperhead! Each was backed against a wall, but the proximity was too much. Dog had been hit. Bolich poked his double down, and with the modified barrel blew off the snake's head. Skinny hiballed off to a neighbor's for a ladder. Dog was retrieved and a dash made for the vet's office.

Luckily, whether because the snake was not very large or because the strike was on a rear leg, remote from the heart, Dog survived to hunt again. But after that he avoided even a garter snake like a plague. He was actually paranoid, and once in a while when hunting, you'd see him jump stiff-legged a foot high for no apparent reason.

George said it was snakes that did it. Here in the South, they are always a threat on warm days.

More wonder, then, at what happened the following summer. Lady saw it, or part of it, from an upstairs window. Beth, almost three, had escaped from the back porch and wandered into the back yard. Dog had dug himself, against all rules, a July-hole amongst the azaleas. The little red wagon, left overturned the day before by the woodpile, was the child's target. Dog, never too enamored of this progeny of the household, stretched, got to his feet, and started to remove himself from the possibility of being loved to death.

It was then he must have seen it. Lady was at that moment flying down the stairs to recapture Beth. Dog, the hated snake-smell in his nostrils and a slithery copper creature coiled almost in front of the child, must have choked on fear. Somehow, he caught the youngster by her ruffled britches, dragging her back. But as Lady dashed through the back door, she saw her child stumble backward and the viper move forward. All she now remembers is that a white streak leaped over the fallen youngster, and there was hell to pay. Dog and snake went round and round, and round, and, well, there was more Dog than snake.

Dog still doesn't like snakes and isn't too fond of girls.

"Cowards die many times before their deaths.
The valiant only taste death but once."
—William Shakespeare

King of Currituck

 was first presented to The King (a.k.a. just plain King) in Judge Godwin's back yard in Raleigh sometime in August in the late sixties. He was one of those short-legged, deep-bodied black Labradors, middle-aged at seven or eight years. Befitting his position as guardian-in-residence of the town house, it was only after introduction by my old friend that the dog came gravely over, sniffed my pantleg, and sat in acceptance of my credentials.

In mid-December, having quickly accepted an invitation to shoot at Currituck, I was watching King plow a furrow in the milfoil off a marsh bank, chasing a crippled widgeon. It was cold enough to make a soprano of the proverbial monkey, but the big dog moved well through the day; not flashy, perhaps, but every inch a solid blind companion and retriever. He dug that crip' out of a muskrat hole and, fighting a chop with ice in its teeth, delivered to hand and climbed back on his stoop by the boat-hide. That was a good day with lots of game, some fair shooting, and exemplary dog work. It was the first of several times I got to hunt with the old man, and at the end of the day King knighted me (although my shooting might not have deserved it) by sidling up in the boat and giving my gloved hand a swipe of his big red tongue. I was instantly counted among his subjects.

Pilston Godwin and I go a long way back, there existing some genealogical intertwinement up the line creating a cousinship of sorts. Bloodline wasn't a necessary ingredient, because in the wonderful way of eastern North Carolina, we'd probably have called each other "cousin" anyway. Temporally, we're peers, both men having now passed seventy. We courted in the same circles, went to law school about the same time, and served in the legislature together. He became a judge and removed his residence from down east to the state capitol. I left the land of my ancestors and moved west to the city. We got together afterward to talk law, literature, politics—and duck shooting. Remarkably, our wives even like each other, a rare boon among hunters.

You see, Pilly had two blinds on the fabulous Currituck Sound. Held by charter from the quasi-governmental and highly autonomous Association, a creature of statute, these were assets money couldn't buy. He also owned the cabin at Grandy, a historic village inhabited almost solely by people of the sea, or rather the sound—a flat, shallow, freshwater body, cut off and protected from its voracious ocean mother by the outer banks of North Carolina.

It's a long haul from my home in the Piedmont, but the company and the ambience of this ancient waterfowl-hunting grounds is too rare a treat to miss. I went when invited.

Remembering other occasions, there was the time son-in-law Pete and I shared the opportunity to hunt with the Judge and King. The dog met us at dockside, scrambled onto the bow of the little Harkers Island motor launch, and in the spitting snow of predawn, formed a frosted figurehead as we motored out to the blind. That day is a memory. I recall making the shot of my life on a lone greenwing jetting on a fifty-yard arc outside the blocks, and King marking down and doing his job in all that weather. Again, bluebills in flocks, suddenly on top of us from out of the snow, and the retriever bringing in, seriatim, six birds from one pass. What a day and what a dog! At night, replete with bourbon, roast duck, and the Judge's absolutely impeccable duck dressing, while King lay in front of the fire, we lied a little about other times and other places, after the manner of duck-hunters everywhere.

The following spring, the Judge with admirable (if unhappy) foresight, acquired a young Chesapeake as heir-in-training and companion for King in his senior years. I liked the pup, who showed promise in yard training, but with perhaps a little excess enthusiasm even for a forty-pound youngster. Pilston was taking the dogs to the coast on weekends for working sessions. We were looking forward to The Season.

It was in late summer, on one of these jaunts, that tragedy struck. Pilly, his voice gruffer than ever on the bench, later told me about it. While free-swimming together in the sound, the dogs got in among the milfoil. The pup, full of ginger and a strong swimmer, wanted to wrestle. The thick weed, the eager pup, the old heart—King drowned.

There is a difference between sentiment and sentimentality. How easy to write a coda that says "The King is dead, long live," etc. What you should know is that the Judge has closed his blinds and sold the cabin. He never told me what he did with the pup. I haven't hunted with him since.

Lewiston

(with apologies to Herbert Jenkins)

he Bertie Ledger-Advance ran a story on page five when Cass Norfleet's pointer disappeared from in front of the drug store in Lewiston. I didn't know about that until way later. I guess bird dogs get lost while hunting, and some never turn up. But the story was that a pointer dog belonging to Norfleet had been trained to stay in the bed of the boss's pickup until released. So when the well-known Pointer wasn't there when Norfleet came out of the store, and found an empty truck, there apparently was Hell to pay. All of this happened way back in the early seventies, but this year I was making a rare visit to cousins in the county, and Cuzz'n Herbert who's a bird hunter with a long memory for bird huntin' stories told me about the mysterious disappearance. And what came after.

It must have been in '71, because my near-grown son and I had been quail hunting with the aforesaid Cuzz'n Herbert while the boy was off from college in the last days of his Christmas vacation. I recall that we had been pretty successful, and that the kid had gotten a legitimate triple on a covey rise, and I was mighty (or as they say in Bertie, "moughty" proud. The following morning we'd hunted a couple of hours and set off toward Rocky Mount and ultimately to Raleigh where I was to drop off the State College junior.

I was then, and still am, living in Asheville, three hundred miles west of the area where we had enjoyed so much the pursuit of *colinus Virginianus* with our favorite kin. I kept only one dog, a setter bitch named Sue, and our departure from Down East came at a fortuitous time, because Sue had just come in heat. That's no condition to have your bird dog in during season, and particularly not in foreign territory. So it was just as well that we were headed home, Sue safely in the dog box in the bed of my F-150.

Well, we had left Aulander at an inconvenient hour, that is, from the boy's point of view. We had worn out breakfast, and had no lunch. So hardly were we wound up to travel, than came the idea of a country ham sandwich or two and that didn't make dad mad either. A drug store is an unlikely source of that delicacy but Lewiston Drug made 'em and the fact was known for miles around. When hunting on the west side of Aulander, that was THE place favored by bird hunters, as was The Quaker House in Woodland when noon found us east of homebase.

On the day said to have been the date of Mr. Norfleet's dog's loss, we were wiping off the ham grease from our lips as we exited to the truck. Imagine our surprise when we found, sitting squarely atop the double dog box, a liver and white pointer. It was pretty obvious that Miss Sue's pheromones had captured his olfactories, which is a high-falutin way of saying the dog had found the lady.

Now I don't dispute the owner's allegations that his dog was wearing a collar with full identification—at least when in his boss's truck. But the dog in my truck damned well didn't have any collar AT ALL. I'm pretty skeptical that any man can train any dog worth his salt to stay in the truck when a breeze wafts toward him the presence of a ready lady lovely in a truck parked next door.

The boy and I promptly de-throned him with a minimum of force, but nevertheless strongly against his will. Of course, we went back inside, but the proprietor had stepped out, so we left our name and alerted some lady about an unmarked dog and drove rather sedately out of town. We were slow about it, because the Ford was missing on one cylinder, and we were debating whether it would get us to Raleigh without changing a plug.

Now Lewiston is not exactly a metropolis, so we really hadn't gone a quarter-mile when The Boy suggested he check to see if the problem was loose wiring. I pulled over to the shoulder of the highway, stopped, and up went the hood for inspection. It was then that I, still inside, saw in the rear vision mirror, what was obviously the pointer, tongue out and loping along behind. The highway west to Oak City is not heavily travelled, but what's there is flying. To leave a good looking lost bird dog at the mercy of that traffic was unthinkable. Having left word with the woman at the store, I, with clear conscience, opened the other side of the dog box, and in jumped the stranger. Later we called him "Lew," for Lewiston, of course.

With the wiring bridle tightened, and all six cylinders humming, and with two frustrated dogs in the rear, we joined the hurrying vehicles headed west. I put a spare collar on the newcomer, bedded both down, separately, in the box for the night in Raleigh, and next day made the long haul home, missing the company of The Boy, but wishing him well in the fractious times of the hippie revolution.

We still had a month of the season, and having heard nothing from the Lewiston area, I kept Lew penned for a week, rubbed him up, petted him and fed him until I thought it safe to take him to the grouse woods. Miss Sue being a setter of impeccable breeding would have to forego her eager suitor, and he, poor fellow, was destined to imposed chastity. The lady being indisposed, I was fortunate to have anything, even a quail dog, to hunt with. The pointer flinched when the first grouse busted out of a laurel hell, but by the end of the second day, he'd about caught on to the difference between small brown bombshells and 105 MM. ruffs. I was delighted, for Lew adapted quickly to close range, and that day and the next, he pointed, held, and retrieved. Hunting alone, I did not need him to back.

My euphoria was short-lived. Before the week was out, Lew failed one day to come in on whistle. We were hunting on the backside of Murphy's Bald, which lies behind Beaucatcher Mountain, not too far from the interstate. I made my way back to the truck as quickly as possible, but no Lew. I almost ran over another truck getting back down the mountain to check at the highway. My shirt, left behind where we'd off-loaded, was still there three days later. Lew had simply disappeared. And I lazily had left on him only the old spare collar with an outdated Asheville dog tag, but no owner's name. I was desolate, sure that he had been stolen or run over.

Here, twenty five years later, riding with Herbert, we visited old haunts. Neither he nor I being the paragons of physical fitness of a quarter century before, and no longer bird hunting, we were reminiscing about the long ago when we stopped, for the first time in years, in Lewiston. It was great to find that country ham still graced the menu. It was then that my companion told about a Mr. Norfleet and his dog's disappearance. In the second week of March that year, a beat-up, bone-thin, "Lew," pads almost worn through and once slick coat tattered, showed up at Norfleet's kennel. And, no doubt about it, still wearing a collar and the Asheville city tag. Norfleet had tried to identify the "thief," but we had moved, and the Asheville tax office simply didn't have time to run down a former dog owner.

So, as that radio man has said forever, "AND NOW YOU KNOW...THE REST...OF THE STORY."

It's one of those miraculous dog-stories that keep popping up—dogs finding their way cross-country, this time almost three hundred miles of territory the pointer had never seen before, nor crossed except locked in a truck dog box. Through cities, over rivers, in and out of traffic!

I have made my apologies to Mr. Norfleet, who kindly accepted some of the blame. It seems he remembered that he, the morning the dog disappeared, had removed the collar to have the nameplate re-bradded. The woman with whom I had left word had simply forgotten to tell her boss about the dog. That the pointer's name was "Stu" and that I called him "Lew" were such sound-alikes that I had no obedience trouble, until—well, until he just wanted to go home. And go home he did!

Writer's NOTE: Based on a mystery reported by Herbert Jenkins of Aulander in his delightful book "Footprints and Memories."

One Man's Justice

One man's justice is another's injustice.—Ralph Waldo Emerson

hrough the mirror on the driver's side, Sandy saw twin tail-lights levitate five hundred yards behind. The lights turned turtle and careened toward the roadside canal. He was crossing Green Swamp, heading west on State 1062 near midnight. Twenty minutes before, he had kissed Cathy goodnight and started for home and bed. Loggers had to be at work at daylight in summer. He was eighteen years old, muscled from his trade like an iron-pumper, and, by reputation, the best young bird hunter in the county.

State 1062 runs fifteen miles through swamp with only a single change of course. About halfway between Dawson, the county seat, and Miller's Store, where

Sandy lived, highway engineers had run into a peat bog so unstable that they had to bend the pavement almost at ninety degrees, squaring up to the bridge over Cypress Creek.

The vehicle that had passed him, going the other way, was doing at least sixty. Even so, Sandy was sure he had recognized Lance Rogers' blue F-250 with its aluminum dog-box. Rogers was older, probably forty, and another quail man. He had recently moved into the neighborhood, down from near Raleigh, he'd said, and had some mighty good-looking dogs the past season. One was a lightly ticked setter bitch, tricolor on her muzzle that bespoke Llewellen, and Sandy had been envious at first sight.

There was not another carlight in sight as Sandy turned his vehicle, having to make two switches on the narrow shoulders, and literally smoked rubber back to the curve. The Ford was upside down, angled nose toward the water, but the cab was still dry. Sandy grabbed the box-lantern from under his seat and slid down the bank to the truck. He could see Lance Rogers, crumpled into the shattered windshield, blood spreading on his arms and shirt. The topside door was jammed shut; the other pinned in the dirt. The boy climbed back, grabbed a peavey from the truck he'd been driving, and in four or five minutes had ripped the door free from the wreck. It was almost too late. He managed to pull the driver free, but there was a long cut on the man's neck, and the blood was pulsing. Sandy had seen plenty of accidents in the logging woods; he found a pressure point, but knew he couldn't hold it and get the man back to a doctor.

It was then that Lance, a gurgle in his voice, said, "Where's Bess? She was in the box. If she's alive, you look after her, and she's yours. And don't let *nobody* take her from you. You know dogs, and she's"—he struggled for breath—"as good as ever walked. Don't let nobody else . . ."

"My God, he's dead!" Sandy said. From somewhere close, he heard a soft whine. The dog-box had been thrown out, and was half submerged. Inside was the tricolor bitch, trying to keep her head above water. Sandy, now bloody and wet to the hips, hoisted out box and dog. The box had fared better than its tenant. Bess, undoubtedly, had a fractured foreleg. With the dog's boss beyond help, the boy threw his jacket over her head, well aware that even good-natured setters may bite when hurt. Cutting a sapling for a splint, he wrapped her leg with his shirt and baling twine. She was calm as he laid her on the floor of his truck.

His CB, at highest volume, only squawked, even on the emergency channel. Then, on 15, a trucker came in, and Sandy passed the word. An hour later three cars had stopped, a state patrolman among them, and an ambulance was on the way. Meanwhile, Bess lay quietly on the floorboard. Later Sandy wondered why he hadn't mentioned her to the folks around. He gave a statement about the wreck and waited until the body was loaded. Then, desperately tired and emotionally drained, he headed for home. But not directly.

Half a mile from his dad's, down a sandy farm lane in a ramshackle cabin, lived an old woman whose father had been a slave. Some called her a conjure-woman because she picked and sold herbs. Sandy laughed at that; he'd known Aunt Sallie all his life. She'd wet-nursed him when he was a baby and still acted as midwife among the poorer folks in the neighborhood. So it was natural, knowing her skills and there being no vet within thirty miles, that he took Bess straight to her. He blew into her yard at three a.m., tooting the horn gently so as not to frighten her, and was met by an apparition in white nightgown and cap and fronted by a double-barreled shotgun.

"That you, Sandy? What you doin' heah in th' middle o' th' night? You hurt?"

On her kitchen table, by oil lamp and flashlight, the leg was set. Bess gave only a sharp yelp as the humerus was pulled and slipped into line, a pair of flat laths applied, a ripped old sheet bound with adhesive tape from the truck's first-aid kit. Sallie set out a bowl of water for her grateful guest and spread her a towsack in the corner for a bed. Then she leaned forward to take a kiss on her wrinkled cheek from her "baby" before pushing him off for home.

It was Saturday, three days later, before Sandy could get off work to take Bess to Doc Blackburn's. Under the X-ray, the bone was so nearly straight that the old man, grumbling about "amateurs," simply rolled on a proper cast and sent them on their way, admonishing Sandy, "Don't, dammnit, try to take that thing off yourself!"

For a month Bess stayed at Aunt Sallie's, sleeping under the porch or idling under one of the chinaberry trees. When the cast was cut off, Sandy still saw no reason to take her home, and the old woman seemed pleased, as much for the dog's company as because her "baby" came over every day or so to bring dogfood or rough up the setter in growing mutual affection. Then the summer job was over, Bess was in the house kennels with Tip and Tuppy, the pointers, and the senior year of high school claimed the boy.

By mid-October, frost had dusted the weedfields and killed the kudzu; snakes weren't much of a threat; scuppernongs and muscadines had given way to persimmons. The season was only six short weeks away. So boy and dogs began the ritual of "working the dogs," meaning up by light, chores completed, and an hour's run through the back pasture up the pine ridge, across the creek, and home to meet the school bus. Bess seemed completely recovered except for a slight knot at the site of the fracture. Shorter in range than the pointers, always checking in, she was as birdy as all get out. And what a sight on point! Head and tail high, her feathers backlighted against a sunrise, she had a style, an elan that spelled breeding with an accent. If her new boss stopped and sat for a breather, she was in his lap loving to be loved; perhaps, in a dog's way, even grateful for what he'd done. And Sandy was no less grateful for what fate had done for him. He seldom thought of Lance Rogers, an unmarried man with no local roots who had lived alone and left no footprints.

The quail season opened the Saturday before Thanksgiving. Sandy and his dad hunted all three school holidays the following weekend. They worked the cut-over soybean fields, the cane bogs, the edges of Green Swamp. The summer weather had been good and birds were plentiful. The dog work was exceptional and Bess was a jewel, having a great nose and impeccable manners. She would find, back, and retrieve, rearing up to return bird-to-hand like nothing seen in that country since Sandy's grandfather's Lil. The world was his oyster and Sandy couldn't have been happier; that is, until *it* happened.

That third Saturday, with Dad busy in town, Sandy went hunting alone. Reveling in her performance, he decided to take only Bess. One man, one dog, he thought. Parking in a logging road on the Johnston place, they quickly moved three coveys, picking up five on the rises and one single. Headed back toward the truck, at the head of a little bay, Bess pointed almost back over her shoulder at a clump of foot-high canes. It was as Sandy moved up that he saw the other two hunters. Their pair of pointers came up and sight-backed. The boy moved in, and on the rise, took two. Bess, amazingly—for though it's been told many times, it rarely really happens—brought in both, her big muzzle lapping with a head hanging out each side. It was a remarkable performance. "Showing off," Sandy said to the newcomers.

"That's a mighty pretty piece of work," said the nearest. Then, in great excitement, the second exclaimed, "Hey, isn't that Lance Rogers' Bess? That sure is.

That's my brother's dog. We thought she was dead or had run off. I'd know her anywhere."

Sandy's heart dropped to his stomach. He started to deny, then explain. But the brother was livid. "Put that dog on this leash, boy. You've got some explaining to do to the law!"

The other man was less strident. "I'm sure the boy can explain. He's probably been to some trouble and expense. Why not give him fifty bucks or so, and we'll be on our way? Besides, you being from Raleigh with the Attorney General's office, I'm sure he wouldn't want to have to go to court."

Sandy was too angry to be intimidated. "Put a hand on that dog, and you'll have me to whip. You got any claim, you just damn prove it in court."

He whistled Bess up on the seat beside him and took off. In the rearview mirror, he saw the brother writing down his license number.

Monday, after school, Sheriff McCauley brought the papers. And it wasn't for a civil action to recover possession of the dog; it was a warrant for larceny. Sandy's dad made bond, and the preliminary hearing was set for the following week. Archie Williamson was to defend. He was supposed to be the best in the district. The case would be presented before old Judge Beachum, hard as nails and the nemesis of all wrongdoers. The local D.A. was embarrassed, but with a prosecuting witness right out of the capital, he had to act tough.

The State then presented the brother, his hunting

companion, and a deputy sheriff from Wake County, all of whom swore that Lance Rogers, now deceased, had owned the setter, that they recognized her as she sat by the court stenographer's desk, that they had hunted over her for two seasons, knew her habits and style, and that two of them had found her in the possession of the defendant, who, upon being accused, fled, with the dog, in a pickup truck, License No. N.C. 4376. The State rested.

Wily old Archie Williamson, figuring no harm could come at this juncture, unprecedentedly asked to put his client on the stand. Normally in this jurisdiction in District Court, there is only State's evidence on the question of whether the defendant is to be bound over to Superior Court. That evidence seemed overwhelming. But the crusty old judge, looking over his half-glasses, said, "Well, I might as well hear what he has to say if his lawyer's fool enough to put him up."

Sandy, badly scared but toughened by his determination not to lose Bess, told his story. Of course, there was no memorandum, no corroborating witness— no real hope. The judge seemed asleep. At the end, when Sandy had told about taking the dog to Aunt Sallie without telling the investigating patrolman about the animal, Lawyer Williamson called his witness down.

The eyes of the judge snapped open. He appeared to be a bit confused as he reached for his gavel, but then he banged it down, and to the amazement of the D.A. and his prosecuting witnesses, he intoned: "I find no probable cause to hold the defendant, and Mister from

Raleigh, this case is ended. Mr. Williamson, bring your client into my chambers."

In chambers, disrobing to show his galluses, and lighting his well-chewed pipe, the judge settled his bottom into the old leather chair and began: "You, young man, are about as surprised as that feller from Raleigh and my bright but misguided young D.A. Let me put you straight. I did not discharge you because I wanted to do you a favor. Not because you're young, nor, especially, because your dad hired this ole reprobate of a lawyer that I'm extremely fond of. There is some background you need to know.

"Twenty or so years ago, a young black boy was in my court accused of stealing a chicken. He had no folks, and I knew he was living in the swamp, raiding farms for something to eat. He'd been caught by a deputy eating a chicken half-cooked over an open fire, and John James' game chicken's feathers were all around him. Now, since old James is the only fellow around here that keeps game cocks—and I later gave him thirty days for fightin' 'em—that boy was guilty as sin. Well, he gave me some story that was a flat-out lie. I said. 'Boy, you can lie about how big a fish you catch, or how many rabbits you catch, or how many girls you bang, 'long as you lie to somebody else. But don't you ever, ever, lie again to this judge.' And I suspended sentence. And he never has—lied, that is—to me since. Asa has been my house man for almost a quarter-century. And since my wife died, he's my best friend."

The lawyer and his client sat silently, wondering if the old man had lost his marbles. He paused a moment, wiped at his eye, and continued. "That's important to you son, in view of what happened today. You see, Asa is still a swamp man. On the night of Lance Rogers' wreck, Asa was coon hunting near where the road crosses Cypress Creek. His dogs had just treed a coon when he heard the truck capsize. He left the dogs at the tree and ran as hard as he could through that mud 'til he came up to you, just as Rogers was telling you to save the dog and you could keep her. But when you said, 'My God, he's dead,' Asa took off. He and his folks aren't much on dead bodies in a swamp.

"So today, I knew you told the truth because you told it just about word for word the way Asa told it to me. And Asa doesn't lie to this judge.

"Now, boy, that dog is getting tired of sitting out there in the court room. Maybe, come Saturday, you'd drop by my house about nine in the morning. I've got about four coveys along the back side of my place, and I'd like to see what all the fuss is about."

Justice Deferred

 got a strange phone call the other day. A male voice asked if I had lived on Radcliffe Avenue in the sixties and had I owned a converted army jeep trailer painted red. My puzzled answer was affirmative. "I just wanted to tell you, I'm the man that stole it, an' I'd like to bring it back," came the confession. Sensing a cleansing of conscience, I told the voice to leave it at a friend's truck yard. And there it appeared, completely rusted out with rotten tires. So much for the crook's good intentions. But the incident put me in mind of another voluntary confession from years and years ago.

Judge Justin Spruill was a fourth generation lawyer in one of those counties in north eastern North Carolina known as the "Chowanoke," a pleasant land of tobacco, soybeans, peanuts, corn, and, of course, quailbirds. I'm talking about the sixties, before the resurgence of cotton as a cash crop when the boll weevil had been conquered. The timing isn't too important, because truth is eternal.

If you have been privileged to read the now out of print "Tutt and Mr. Tutt" stories by the late Arthur Trane, you have a picture of Judge Spruill—not like the principle hero Mister Tutt, but on the order of his sibling, Tutt. Our judge was like Tutt—short, round, pink, and jovial. As Mr. Tutt loved fly-fishing, Justin Spruill loved bird-hunting. But he yielded to no man his love for his territory, his people, and his dogs. And the people knew him as a fair but tough lower court judge, where he had picked up the title, and in later years, as a brilliant and fiery trial lawyer.

As with most of the species, he had spent term after term in the Legislature, leading his party in humane recognition of the rights and desires of the less fortunate, and earning a reputation as an orator unmatched since the days of Zeb Vance. His long service had made him a master of parliamentary procedures, but he had finally turned the post over to a young fellow from an adjoining county, so he could devote more time to his recently acquired passion, which was running dogs in field trials.

The shortage of bobwhite in the once bosom of the shooting sport had brought on this secondary recognition of quality pointers and setters. (In this territory, no versatiles need apply.) And Judge Spruill had gone head over heels into the competition, enlarging his kennels, seeking out new blood, breeding for speed, and training and handling his own candidates. His accumulated two thousand or so acres of row crops were augmented by cut-overs and swampland, ideal for scientific attempts to bring back *colinus Virginians,* while at the same time offering the greatest of training grounds for his dogs.

There were not many field trials in his part of the state, so most of the action tended to be down toward the sandhills, culminating at the big shows at Hoffman. But meanwhile, a number of non-accredited fun trials were being run within fifty miles or so, and it was a sight to see the rotund little man mounted on a pure white gelding whooping on his entries. He had devised a system of two stirrups on the near-side, one with straps long enough for his short leg to reach while he huffed and puffed his way to the converted McClelland Calvary saddle his grandfather had taken from a fallen Union officer in the War.

By now I should have told you about Dan, the call name for Spruill's Dashing Dan, Llewellin setter of the first order, and apple of the judge's eye. A three year old tri-color, mid-size at forty-five pounds, he combined the speed of smaller dogs with the power of a larger pointer. He was one "ragin' fireball," as characterized by the judge's old friend Ennis Benthall, who frequently rode "scout" during trials. Dan was mopping up in the local competition, and was known as the dog-to-beat since he had aged into the shooting dog class. His boss limited his practice to trial work, usually in association with a forwarding lawyer, and since court terms were relatively sporadic, and with no commitments in Raleigh where the Legislature had begun sitting near the first of January, the winter and spring of sixty-six bade fair to be a great time for the new activity.

Ah, but man's good fortune is not guaranteed. Upon the horizon of happiness, dark clouds appeared. Into the next county moved, from the sandhills country, one Elmer Scroggs, lawyer of sorts, and dedicated pointer man. Rumor had it that Scroggs had figured in some sort of scam involving substitution of dogs sold by him—delivered dogs being other than the ones shown a customer. But the alleged villain joined a neighboring field trial club and entered two puppies, a derby, and the most handsome lemon pointer seen in those parts in many a day. The man knew dogs! And his Jake knew how to win.

I do not have space here to detail the rivalry between our Judge and Scroggs, for the latter was a cagey, shrewd. and often successful lawyer, gaining a reputation among those prospective litigants who would use the courts for causes not always compatible with true justice. But the battles, both in court and in the field were memorable and the dining room at Quaker House filled with new stories of the encounters. The men developed a less than cordial relationship and made certain to avoid each other, especially at the lunches shared by all the others of the Courthouse crowd at Woodland.

Having reported the conflict necessary to a good story, I must next relate a sort of semi-climax. It came at a regional trial held in the judge's county, pumped up by the prospect of viewers seeing Dan finally going head- to-head with Scrogg's Jake. They had both been called back after running their respective braces, and were set to go right after lunch. At the "Loose your dogs," from the judges, the pointer flew left down a beanfield, while the setter took the edge above a swamp. Both were flying.

Then occurred the unbelievable! Dan, who was broke to the whistle, failed to turn on the judge's signal. Repeated, there was no response. Dan simply kept going, out of sight and off course. Scroggs, grinning like a 'possum, picked up the trophy and quickly departed. Ennis Benthall and Judge Spruill, joined by half a dozen puzzled cronies, searched until dark. No Dan. Nor was subsequent effort rewarded in the following weeks despite advertising, even on the radio. The would-be champion had simply disappeared. The heart-broken judge withdrew from trialling, although he did foot-hunt a bit on occasion.

It was four years later that, while so hunting with a younger man, Judge Spruill saw a pick-up truck cutting across the field so as to intercept the hunters. Inside was of all people, Elmer Scroggs. "Now, hold on, Judge," he said. "I ain't armed and am lookin' for no fight. But my wife made me go with her to hear Billy Graham, and I've found the Lord. I'm a changed man, born again, and a matter is on my conscience. I'm responsible for your Dan's running off. At lunch that day, I walked up to your stake-out. Nobody was around, so I pretended to pet your dog. I stuck some bubble gum in each ear, and of course, knew he couldn't hear you. After he disappeared, and while the mob was searching for him, I intercepted him running back to your truck, took him to my place in Virginia, and only hunted him, never trialled him for fear of getting caught. He died last night, and I've brought you the collar and seek your Christian forgiveness."

Carefully Judge Spruill broke his Parker side-by-side, and dropped the shells in the pocket of his hunting coat. Then the little man, like a bantam rooster, his chest swelling and his hands shaking with fury, with rising voice said, "Mr. Scroggs, as a law-abiding man, I have unloaded to keep myself from killing you. I'm not a forgiving man and in a not forgiving mood. I'll have you in court and have your license, you lying, thieving, blackguard!"

But the crafty new-comer said, "Now you know that I can't be guilty of stealin' because a dog not listed for taxes is not 'property' an' I done checked the listing an' you ain't never paid no taxes on Dan, an'—an' you ain't got no case at all."

"Just a minute, Scroggs, you are not only a thief, but a damned sorry lawyer to boot. I have no hope of teaching you any law. However, the common law rule that dogs weren't subject to larceny was altered by the Act of 10 George three hundred years ago, and that's followed by almost every state in the Union except Louisiana, whether a dog is tagged or not.

I didn't list Dan because Dan was not my dog. This young man with me is my step-son. When I married his mother, a dozen years ago, I found I also loved her boy, Joe, who bears his father's name of Yates. When he was eighteen, I gave Dan to him, and he did the tax-listing in his own name. I did Dan's training because this boy was himself in training—at the State Law Enforcement School at Salemburg. You are going to see a lot of him so I ought to introduce Deputy Sheriff Yates."

Scroggs, temporarily set back, swiftly recovered. "You still can't do nothin' about it because it's been more than three years, and the statute of limitations bars you, so go tuck it!"

"Oh no, Mr. Scroggs. You see I still have some friends left in Raleigh. I knew somebody stole Dan and he'd show up someday. We sneaked through a little local bill for my county only, extending for five years the statute of limitation on dog stealing. There is still another year to go.

Take him into custody, Mr. Sheriff. I'll sign the warrant at the Courthouse."

Note: See Scharfield vs. Richardson, 133 F2 340 for a summary of state laws regarding status of dogs as personal property whether or not tax listed. First recognized in this country in Meig's Case, 1 MacArthur 53 (DC).

Chief of Whiteoak Pocosin

I'm sitting here on the balcony of a rather posh hotel overlooking the Atlantic, and it's 1979, and I wonder about life and living, and all the complexities that go with it. And about how I happen to be here, with a forty dollar a day room when I only make sixty-five dollars a week.

My daddy would have been a hundred years old this year (he died in sixty-eight). And Uncle Alfred, golly, he was at Pickett's charge in the War Between the States, but after the war he lived with Papa Joe and Grandma 'til Daddy was maybe eighteen. So the stories he told came down to me through three generations, and I guess maybe I'll tell my kid, if I ever I have any, some of them.

Like the story of the white stag that lived in Whiteoak pocosin. If any of you readers have gotten this far without knowing what a pocosin is, it is roughly defined as a swamp located on ground higher than the general area.

Frequently thick and impenetrable, pocosins usually hold game. And there are clearings and savannahs where walking hunting is not impossible.

Daddy was born there on the edge of Whiteoak, and the nearest sort of settlement was Deppe, up the road from Jacksonville, which is the county seat. The whole family farmed and timbered for a living, but hunted and fished for fun and sustenance. None was educated until my dad's generation. He went off to Richland school, where he later taught, and then to the University, where he got his law degree. As a youngster, he financed this schooling by splitting fence-rails, and was said to have once split 500 in a day—county champion. Those were my kind of folks.

To put this in a time frame, Daddy told me that Papa Joe had told him that Uncle Alfred's story of the ghost deer began shortly after the surrender. He had come home from the war, and was hunting one October day, when he got lost in the pocosin just as the sun went down. He knew he was in for a cold and hungry night, and was making a fire in front of a hollow beechtree where he planned to sleep out of the wind. It was then that Indian Eddie showed up. He looked, Uncle Alfred said, to be a century old, all wrinkled and stooped, and dressed mostly in deerskin and wearing moccasins. Everybody around Deppe knew, or knew of, Eddie. Rumor had it that there had always been Indians in the swamps, ever since the Tuscarora War in the early seventeen-hundreds. You remember, that was when the whites from around New Bern had sought help from South Carolina, and five hundred fighters came to drive the once mighty Tuscarora tribe back to New York.

Most school children in eastern Carolina, back when they were taught state history, and before "social studies," knew about the wonderful adventures of John Lawson. He was an Englishmen who had walked all the way from Charleston almost to Charlotte, and then back to the coast. He had written a journal that was an amazing account of how he travelled among the Indians, and how he described the animals and birds. What we always thought was funny was that he called snakes, alligators, and turtles "inseckts." And we all held our breaths when we got to the story of how he and Baron DeGraffenried, who founded New Bern, went west looking for new lands, and the very Indians Lawson had been friends with, killed him. That was when we heard they stuck splinters of lightwood under the fingernails and set them on fire. The girls in the class always shivered, and some of us just had to put an arm around and comfort them.

Some Indian descendants remained in the state, and over in Robeson County they were numerous, owning their own land, and some being grey-eyed, were thought to go back to the lost English colony from the barrier island on the coast. Anyway, Indian Eddie of Whiteoaks shortly after the Civil War was a fact, not fiction. And that night when he brought out his cooking pot, and made up a rabbit and squirrel stew thickened with chinquapin nuts, Uncle Alfred was mighty pleased. He later said that Eddie had told him about an all-white buck deer that frequented that same section of the pocosin, and wondered what its hide would bring if anybody ever killed it.

It was the next Fall that the Indian, (who somehow, since he talked so little, spoke pretty good English) let slip at Eubank's store that he had really killed the Phantom buck. He was curing the skin, and inquired where he could get the best price. He said he'd bring the hide in "next week" and wanted "at least ten dollars" for it. Word like that gets around in a small community, and at a time when coonskins brought thirty-five cents, and a red-fox pelt only brought a dollar, ten dollars seemed like a fortune. Folks have been killed for less.

So, when Eddie didn't show up by the following Saturday, Uncle Alfred and Sam Aman went into the pocosin to Eddie's cabin. There on the floor, his head split open with an axe, lay the old man. There had been no effort to bury his remains, and, of course, no sign of a white deer hide. Uncle Alfred said the corpse had begun to stink, so he and Sam dug a grave in the little clearing and marked it with a heart-pine board on which they burned just the name "Eddie" and the date. Papa Joe always said, "Them Walkers done it." The Walker brothers had joined up with the red-shirts but only used the membership as a cover for all kinds of meanness. But nobody ever proved it on them.

After the war, a lot more people seemed to live in the area. At least there were a lot more hunters in the woods, maybe just trying to eke out a living during the reconstruction days. But about every two or three weeks, somebody would come in with the report of seeing a huge white stag with "rockin' chair" rack, slipping ghostily though the swamps, or flying over fallen timber "six feet high." Then the story expanded. Now the stag had a rider, an old Indian with wrinkled face and buckskin shirt. It was said that the great deer left off its rider in rutting season and spent its time and energy looking for a white doe, no ordinary female being attractive to, nor worthy of, the "Chief of Whiteoak," as he had become known to the locals. It got so nobody would go into that part of the woods, and the vision became part of the culture and history of the region for the neat four generations.

I had come back from Nam with such a negative attitude, it's a wonder I wasn't locked up for good. I mustered out, as the Brits say, at Norfolk, and promptly drank my way into a couple of Virginia's nastiest jail cells. I did seasonal work up and down the coast, especially along Currituck, where I set eel traps for the Japanese, netted shrimp for the tourists at Kitty Hawk, and even guided for ducks and geese out of Poplar Branch. I had always been handy with the smooth bores, and I bluffed my way among the Barcoses and Midgettes, and Davises, pretending I had been raised south on Core Banks before going into the service. Having no boat and no money, I helped one of the Whitsons that I won't name because I'd embarrass a fine gentleman. I'm sure he caught on to my lying, but he had been in WWII, and had seen some of his buddies have the same kind of shakes I used to get at night. I did get some experience, and I learned that weather cold enough to make a soprano of the brass monkey wouldn't kill you if you worked. And that there were some decent people in the world who'd like to be nice to you if you'd only let them. And that hunting and fishing were two things I wanted to do for the rest of my life. But the shakes were hard to get rid of. It took four long, difficult years.

I was still single, having retained enough decency not

to impose on some girl a misanthropic nomad who sometimes hated the world, and acted accordingly. Somehow, though, some sunshine broke through my cloud cover, I kicked myself in the butt, sobered up, and decided the time had come to get back in the world.

Here more than a century after Uncle Alfred, I had returned to the land of my fathers, as the historians say. Back in Onslow, where I was kin to the Shepards, Hendersons, Amans, Eubankses, Mortons, and most everybody else, I had taken a job with Texas Gulf as an office clerk, with just enough supervisory authority to earn my sixty-five a week. But it was nine to five and weekends off, and I could hunt and fish in what was once a wildlife paradise.

At first I lived at the motel at Maysville, but when I got a dog, I had to move out. So I rented a clap-board house that had been left vacant when the military tenant got shipped out. I fenced a pen and, for the cost of the county license and a five buck fee, picked Sandy out from the local pound. He was what I called a "drop," meaning he looked about half pointer-half setter, but certainly some sort of bird dog. I had noticed him pointing sparrows through the fence so thought that, since he was just an adolescent, he might learn the quail game. Turned out that he had some natural pointing ability, but had learned some bad habits. Or what would have been unacceptable to a solid bird hunter. The fact that he flushed rabbits, barked at treed squirrels, pointed quails and retrieved anything smaller than he was made him ideal, at least for me. I would learn that the British call this a "rough shooting dog"—one that would do it all. And Sandy was certainly rough. But we had grown friendly, and ultimately affectionate with one another, and I was glad to have him share my loneliness.

Sometimes I hunted with Jody Eubanks whom I had known in grammar school. Jody and I would explore the pocosin, killing a couple of bucks every season, taking friends a turkey at Thanksgiving, and having a mess of Bobwhites for supper most nights during season. But mostly, I was still a loner, and the dog was company enough. Every so often I thought I saw an all white deer, but never close enough for a shot. I didn't tell anybody, not even Jody, because a fellow could look awfully silly talking about seeing a hundred-year old deer.

For a while there I hunted and fished every free minute. I read recently that a feller was bragging on his dog, saying that if he picked up his .22, the dog would run to the squirrel woods; his twenty-gauge, and off to the bean fields for birds; the rifle took the dog to the deep woods to flush out a deer. Well, Sandy was at least that smart. And I always carried several loads—sixes, eights, and a couple of 00 buckshot, because I never knew what we were to find, from Canadas to coons.

A month ago, in early deer season, Sandy and I had ventured deeper into Whiteoak pocosin than I had intended. I had taken a rough compass course in invading this place, so I was not entirely lost, although I didn't recognize my exact location, when Sandy gave a yip and took off to run a deer. It was almost dark, and I wanted to get back to civilization before nightfall, so I hollered him back. Now any deerhunter knows that wily old bucks aren't always spooked by a commotion, but sometimes lie doggo until a opportunity for escape is offered. Which is what happened. Sandy came in, and promptly pointed a thicket of haw and myrtles. But I had already loaded the old Ithaca double twelve with the buckshot, and before I could shift to the eights for possible quail, out roared the greatest buck I had ever seen. It had a coat-rack of at least ten points, and it was ALL WHITE. Not albino. The eyes were dark as coffee cups as it busted the myrtle bushes on the edge of the tree line. He was in the open for, maybe, thirty yards, so I saw him clearly. It was automatic, my swinging the gun to bear on his neck, and the second barrel took him behind the right shoulder.

I was lucky to be loaded with the big stuff, I thought, and set off at once to follow a blood trail. Sandy, however, hung back, and I could hardly drag him to the fresh scent which must have been just left. As a matter of fact, he struggled so hard I pulled off his collar, at which he dropped his tail and slunk away like he 'd been whipped. Not having time to mess with a crazy dog, I pushed through a wall of brush, and in the growing darkness, I spotted, fifty yards away under a pine, the shape of a downed deer. With sheath knife drawn, I dropped to my knees to bleed the buck.

IT WASN'T THE BUCK! This was a hundred ten pound doe, and she WAS TOTALLY WHITE. What about the rack I'd seen? The huge male with knotted neck in mid-rut? The very deer whose "ghost" had been around for a century? Gone! All gone!

Totally shell-shocked, I put my hunting cost under her hips so as to save the hide, and dragged her in darkness half a mile to the jeep. I sold the hide to Smithsonian as a rare and unprecedented non-albino, all-white Virginia type Eastern whitetail for exhibition purposes. I took the five-hundred bucks, quit the clerkship, and came here to wonder: Had I been nuts when I saw the stag in all his glory? Was there any buck at all? Do you really believe in ghosts? Do I?

I called room service. "Send up another bourbon and water, double Daniels, please."

Footnote: In the ensuing fifteen or so years, no one in the Deppe community has reported seeing the "Chief of Whiteoak pocosin." The story is totally fiction, though the names of my folks in the area, which I dearly love, are real.

Quitter?

he business card had shown:

APOGEE CORPORATION

John Foote Oliver, President and CEO

Computer Consultants   Atlanta, GA

That was a couple years back, when John was rolling high and before the fire. The fire had been at the stables where his wife Sallie and ten year old daughter Joanie had been swamping stalls for the child's first love, a Tennessee walker named "Brighteyes." Nobody ever found what caused it. The disaster was devastating—all dead in five minutes of flaming horror. John had fought on for a while, then sold the business, burying himself in his grief, and wallowing in self-pity.

He played a few rounds with old friends at the club, but never lingered for socializing. Once in a while, he'd hunt quail over somebody else's dogs, not daring to make himself vulnerable even to losing a beloved dog. Nights were spent reading or blindly watching stupid TV sitcoms—at which he almost never laughed. Without a salary, he drew on capital from the stock sale. He was a miserable rag of a human being.

Thus it was that day after golf—he'd shot an unsatisfactory 80—that Perrin stopped by the locker. They were not particularly good friends; mostly just fellows who occasionally golfed together. "John," he said. "I hear you used to be something of a bird hunter. I'd like to invite you to go with me down to my brother's place in Alabama for three or four days. Frankly, I thought Jim Estill was going, but he's backed out. Come on. We'll have some fun, and you look as though you could use some."

The first reaction was predictably negative. "I don't want to go anywhere. Don't know his brother. Don't want to birdhunt," he thought. But hell, it was December and Christmas just around the corner, and he was alone, alone. alone. He started to make excuses, but then succumbed to the blandishments of his proposed companion whose wit and charm had earned him scores of friends.

"Tell me about it," he inquired.

"Well, you just dig out your old huntin' stuff, some good walkin' boots, although we may be riding a lot, and bring your gun. We'll stay with Rob and Cynthia— they're older than I—and we'll pick up licenses and shells at the store. Weather's likely to be warm, but take a heavy jacket just in case.

I've got to go by New Orleans, so I'll have to ask you

to drive and meet me there. You'll have a marked map in your locker tomorrow."

John almost withdrew. He really had no enthusiasm for an out of state birdhunt, nor, he thought, for most anything else. Life was dull and drab, and here at forty six, hardly worth the effort. He felt a bit better the following Tuesday, the day set, when he pulled on some old briar britches and found them comfortable. His Browning waterproofs needed oiling. And the Parker double 20 gauge he'd inherited from his father swung smoothly through a dry-firing. But in the night, the ghosts came back—his girls spinning in the smoke and flames—until he cried out and rolled out of bed onto the cold floor. "Why not," he considered, "just take the 20 gauge and…?"

Morning though, found him headed west, his ten year old Ferrari humming toward Independence, nestled in the red clay hills in the north part of the neighboring state. He was surprised to find that this was not cotton country, but vast pastureland, interspaced with forty-foot wide mock orange windbrakes. "Where is any bird cover?" he mused.

Consulting now the hand drawn map that took him from the paved highway, he began looking for the plantation mansion. Instead, at the mailbox marked with Rob's name, he could see, set back from the road, a simple, white two-story residence, fairly modern in the fifties, but with no visible pretenses. It was late afternoon after his drive from Atlanta, and he thought he might even be in time for a bourbon.

Stopping in the gravelled drive and beginning to off load, standing with guncase in hand and car door open, he had surprisingly noticed a bright red little Eagle Summit wagon alongside. Just at that moment, out from the front door of the house came a matching red dress, draped curvaceously over what must have been a delicious body, topped by a short-cut hairdo, and graced by a pair of gray eyes, set wider apart than any he'd ever seen. "Hi and bye," the creature said as she slipped into the Eagle and spun out of the driveway.

Perrin having arrived somewhat earlier, the two visitors were greeted warmly by Rob and wife, offered potables proper for a frosty evening, and sumptuously fed country ham, grits, collards, hot biscuits, and blackberry pie, all proceeding from a kitchen presided over by Ella, large, black, white aproned, and jolly. Next morning, John was awakened by a rustle as a shadowy figure appeared to be building a fire in the fireplace of his upstairs room. "Howdy, suh. I'se Lonzo an' will be lookin' afta you this week." And so it was. The ubiquitous Alonzo became a smiling black face to hold a stirrup, pass up a shotgun, hold the horse for covey rises, and open gates as riding hunters covered twenty-five to thirty miles a day. A kennel of Selma-bred pointers flooded out, sometimes half a mile in front, holding like stones until the entourage rode up. The birds were feeding under the mock orange, and John learned to slip quickly off horse, take his Parker from Alonzo, step up to the line and found his one-time skills quickly returning. Several times he doubled; on they moved to another covey.

"This may not be Tara," John thought, "but it may be the last surviving working plantation."

It was, however, the pointers, and particularly Rob's lead dog Tony, that set John drooling. Never had he seen such flawless perfection, and he realized that such paragons of performance must cover, in front of horses, at least a hundred twenty five miles a day! Almost he wanted such a dog—and a chance to get back into quailing.

It was late in the afternoon, just at dusk, when Tony ran a three-inch mock orange thorn clear through his right forefoot. Alonzo picked him up, pulled the thorn, and Rob poured over the paw part of the contents of a silver flask he mysteriously pulled from some inner pocket. Headed anyway back to the 8 foot fenced kennel (bird dogs are inveterate climbers) which Rob had installed in his backyard, the huntsmen followed Alonzo and his charge to be put in until the healing could take place. It was a loss to John, who had come to admire Tony more than any bird dog he'd ever seen.

Next day was the last, and the hunt went on with the addition of a neighboring land owner of some eighty years, partially paralyzed in one arm, and seemingly permanently mounted on a white gelding. He shot from the saddle, and killed twenty birds on his own amazing production. The morning was halfway over, when from the rear there exploded the irrepressible Tony, running on three legs, but not to be denied his hunt. Over the chain-link fence he had come to his place as number one. John almost cried in emotional response to the great dog's effort.

His forebearer, the late John Taintor Foote, writer extraordinaire of fine dog stories, would certainly have made something of this episode, John thought. It was a few days worthy of recording, and he wished for his great uncle's talents.

But, with a dozen frozen quail packed in ice, a warm

invitation to return, and the Ferrari humming east, the young man faced again the black despair that had followed him for almost three years. It wrapped around him as he unlocked the apartment with no greeting from beast nor human. "Hell," he thought, "I ought to just throw in the towel."

Then two things happened. A call from a former associate saying a new consulting firm was being formed and they'd like John to manage it. To this he promised to "think about it" overnight. The second was devastating. A telegram from Rob. It said, "Tony died today. We chained him inside the pen to protect his foot. He went over anyway and hanged. You would want to know he never quit. Regards."

John dropped his head in anguish. Then suddenly he jumped up, piled into the Ferrari, and at the Western Union telegraph station sent two wires. First to the business associate, "Accepted." Second to Rob and Cynthia. "Do you have room first week in January? Identify girl in red Eagle."